YES WE CAN!

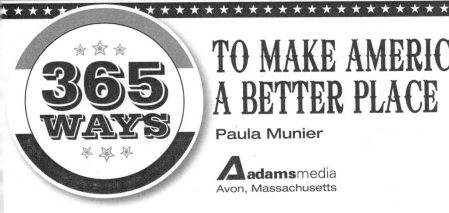

365 WAYS

TO MAKE AMERICA A BETTER PLACE

Paula Munier

▲ adamsmedia
Avon, Massachusetts

Published by
Adams Media, a division of F+W Media, Inc.
57 Littlefield Street, Avon, MA 02322. U.S.A.
www.adamsmedia.com

ISBN 10: 1-4405-055-X
ISBN 13: 978-1-4405-0055-8

Printed in Canada.

J I H G F E D C B A

Library of Congress Cataloging-in-Publication Data
is available from the publisher.

This publication is designed to provide accurate and authoritative information
with regard to the subject matter covered. It is sold with the understanding that
the publisher is not engaged in rendering legal, accounting, or other professional advice. If legal advice or other expert assistance is required, the services
of a competent professional person should be sought.
  —From a *Declaration of Principles* jointly adopted by a Committee of the
American Bar Association and a Committee of Publishers and Associations

Many of the designations used by manufacturers and sellers to distinguish their
product are claimed as trademarks. Where those designations appear in this
book and Adams Media was aware of a trademark claim, the designations have
been printed with initial capital letters.

♣ The pages of this book are printed on 100% post-consumer recycled paper.

Megaphone art © istockphoto/Nemanja Pesic
Microphone art © istockphoto/bubaone

This book is available at quantity discounts for bulk purchases.
For information, please call 1-800-289-0963.

Yes We Can!

CONTENTS

★ ★

★ ★

PART
ONE

KEEP
AMERICA
WEALTHY

CHAPTER 1 **WORK SMARTER** 9	**1.** Help a laid-off worker find a new job. 9	**2.** Write a letter of reference for an out-of-work employee. 10
3. Recommend someone for a job. 10	**4.** Start a cottage industry on the side. 11	**5.** Hire local workers to support that cottage industry. 11
6. Devise strategies to boost productivity. 11	**7.** Boost your own productivity at work. 12	**8.** Start an internship program for local college students. 12
9. Teach an unskilled laborer a marketable skill. 13	**10.** Moonlight. 13	**11.** Be a mentor. 13
12. Sit on the board of a company. 14	**13.** Hire a kid to do your yardwork or fix your computer. 14	**14.** Give a teen a summer job. 15

15.

Donate interview clothes to a local women's shelter.

15

16.

Join the chamber of commerce.

16

17.

Invent something.

16

18.

Join SCORE.

16

CHAPTER 2

SPEND SMARTER

17

19.

Pay off all your credit card debt.

17

20.

Buy local.

18

21.

Spread the word about your favorite local businesses.

18

22.

Buy American.

19

23.

Repay your student loans.

19

24.

Keep a money log.

20

25.

Comparison shop online.

20

26.

Reprogram your money mindset.

21

27.

Raise your credit score.

21

28.

Pay your bills on time.

22

29.

Speak up about poor service or workmanship.

22

30.

Negotiate for better terms on your mortgage.

23

31.

Negotiate for better terms on your credit cards.

23

32.

Sign up for automatic payment plans.

24

33.

Avoid buying new retail products.

24

34.

Establish an emergency fund.

25

35.

Bargain everywhere for everything.

25

36.

Make a budget— and stick to it.

26

CHAPTER 3

SAVE SMARTER

27

37.

Save 10 percent of your salary.

27

38.

Switch banks if your bank took bailout money and won't report how it's spending it.

28

39.

Switch firms if your investment brokerage firm took bailout money and won't report how it's spending it.

28

40.

Set up a living trust.

29

41.

Invest in yourself.

29

42.

Invest in your community.

30

43.
Invest in your nation.

30

44.
Neither a borrower nor a lender be.

31

45.
Save all your change and bank it.

31

46.
Postpone your retirement.

32

47.
Rent out a room to someone who's lost their home.

32

48.
If you're married, try to stay that way.

33

49.
Live with someone and share expenses.

33

CHAPTER 4

FIGHT CORPORATE GREED

35

50.
Become a whistleblower.

35

51.
Boycott companies that outsource jobs overseas.

36

52.
Outsource to local businesses.

36

53.
Support your local union.

37

54.
Support a minimum wage increase.

37

55.
Report egregious corporate policies to a TV station.

38

56.
Shoot a documentary about local corporate greed.

38

57.
Write an editorial for your local newspaper.

38

58.
Protest bait-and-switch tactics.

39

59.
Launch an e-mail campaign against unfair practices.

39

60.
If your company spends taxpayer money on parties, etc., refuse to participate.

40

61.
If your company spends taxpayer money on parties, etc., alert the media.

40

62.
Boycott companies that offer golden parachutes.

41

CHAPTER 5

FIGHT GOVERNMENT WASTE

43

63.
Keep an eye out for government waste.

43

64.
Alert the media if you encounter government waste.

44

65.
Start an e-mail campaign against instances of government waste.

45

66.
Stage a sit-in to protest fiscal irresponsibility at your town hall.

45

67.
Vote against spendthrift budget items at your town hall meetings.

45

68.
Vote for fiscally responsible candidates.

46

69.
Write an editorial for your local newspaper.

46

70.
Blog about wasteful spending.

46

71.

Note instances of government waste and post them online.

47

72.

Contact a local TV reporter if you encounter wasteful government spending.

47

73.

Sign a petition for waste-cutting propositions.

48

74.

Support legislation to regulate Wall Street.

48

75.

Support legislation to regulate the banking industry, too.

48

WORK SMARTER

1 Help a laid-off worker find a new job.

Massive layoffs have plagued us from coast to coast. The hardest-hit industries: construction and manufacturing. The hardest-hit regions of our nation: the West and the Midwest. But Americans from California to Florida, from all walks of life, are losing their jobs. Everyone knows someone who just got laid off. So adopt one of these unemployed workers and dedicate yourself to helping that person land a new position. If you think there's nothing you can do, think again. Encourage your unemployed friends and family members by helping them:

★ Update their resume
★ Search for jobs online
★ Approach colleagues and industry insiders
★ Network within their respective field
★ Identify opportunities outside their field
★ Put out feelers with your own contacts
★ Prepare for interviews
★ Stay motivated with pep talks as needed

enough!
At 6.5 percent, the unemployment rate is higher than it's been in fourteen years. According to the *Washington Post*, some economists expect the rate could very well top 8 percent, which would be the highest we've seen in a generation.

CALL TO
Online Action!

Top Five Job Search Websites
Monster.com
Indeed.com
FedWorld.org
CareerBuilder.com
Dice.com

Source: *http://websearch .about.com*

2 Write a letter of reference for an out-of-work employee.

Letters of recommendation can make or break a job search. Employers typically ask candidates for three such letters of recommendation; more important, they do check them out. So one of the most useful things you can do for an out-of-work colleague is write a winning commendation of their talents, skills, and experience. The best-prepared job seekers present letters of recommendation tailored to the position they desire; ask colleagues what they'd like you to focus on in your letter. Write the best recommendation you can—the next recommendation you may need may be your own.

3 Recommend someone for a job.

When it comes to finding a job, *who you know* beats Monster.com any day. In fact, three out of four jobs are not advertised at all, as many employers prefer hiring people they know, or know of. Recommending colleagues for a job may be the shortcut to the paycheck they've been waiting for. Better yet, many companies reward employees who recommend new hires. Ask your human resources department about your company's recommendation policy.

friends don't let friends find a job alone

According to the Department of Labor, most Americans find a job through personal contacts. The top ways people find a job:

48 percent, friends or family
24 percent, cold calling (no ad posted)
23 percent, alumni or school placement professionals
5 percent, newspaper or website ads

4 Start a cottage industry on the side.

Enterprising Americans start more than half a million businesses every month, according to the Ewing Marion Kauffman Foundation. It's this spirit of entrepreneurship that makes our nation the most innovative on earth. From Mrs. Field's Cookies to YouTube cofounders Chad Hurley and Steve Chen, success stories abound. So why not join the ranks of these profit-minded small business people—and turn a little profit of your own?

5 Hire local workers to support that cottage industry.

Founding and running your own business is as American as Mrs. Smith's Apple Pie. Most Americans work for small companies; so when you hire people to help you run your new business, you're helping the economy as well as your bottom line.

6 Devise strategies to boost productivity.

The quickest and often most effective way to boost productivity is to go right to your workforce. Ask employees to suggest improvements, and reward them for the most useful strategies.

Rallying Cry!

"Tens of millions of families are struggling to figure out how to pay the bills and stay in their homes."

— BARACK OBAMA

CALL TO
Online Action!

Top Five Small Business Websites

www.sba.org

www.abwa.org

www.entrepreneur.com

www.score.org

www.inc.com

small is $mart

Some 66 percent of Americans work for companies with fewer than 250 employees, according to the U.S. Department of Labor. Small businesses employ 50.9 percent of all nonfarm workers in the private sector.

> *"Productivity is being able to do things that you were never able to do before."*
>
> — FRANZ KAFKA

7 Boost your own productivity at work.

With unemployment on the rise, you want to make sure you hold onto your job—even if everyone around you is losing theirs. That means boosting your productivity—and hence your value to your company. Here are ten ways to increase your effectiveness:

1. Eliminate distractions.
2. Make a to-do list daily.
3. Skip unnecessary meetings.
4. Get caller ID to cut down on needless phone calls.
5. Do the tedious/tough/boring stuff first.
6. Only check your e-mail twice a day.
7. No web surfing.
8. Delegate.
9. Outsource.
10. Love what you do.

enough!

The biggest time waster in the typical office is meetings, according to a survey by *Executive's Briefcase.*

8 Start an internship program for local college students.

Student interns are 1) cheap and 2) motivated. For the price of an honorarium, they get experience—and you get people to whom you can delegate virtually any task. . . . Not to mention potential entry-level new hires! Contact your local community college, and ask for the head of the department most likely to provide you with the skill set you need.

interned!

Nearly three in every four college students work as interns before graduation, according to Vault, Inc. A whopping 55 percent of these interns receive no pay.

9 Teach an unskilled laborer a marketable skill.

With outsourcing on the rise and manufacturing jobs moving overseas, unskilled workers often find themselves underemployed or unemployed altogether. Take such a worker under your wing, and teach him or her whatever marketable skills you can. Particularly valuable: verbal and written communication skills; general computer skills, as well as software know-how; technical expertise; organizational skills; and administrative skills.

THE PRESIDENT SAYS

"The business of America is business."

— CALVIN COOLIDGE

10 Moonlight.

11 Be a mentor.

Hone your leadership skills while you help a younger, less experienced colleague up the ladder of success in your given field. You can also groom your protégé to become your right-hand person—or even your successor. Remember: You can't move up yourself until you've got someone ready to take on your former responsibilities. Mentor well, and your protégé might just fit the bill.

"I considered Nat King Cole to be a friend and, in many ways, a mentor. He always had words of profound advice."

— DIAHANN CARROLL

12 Sit on the board of a company.

In many companies, the true power is held by the board members. Power corrupts, as the Enrons and the Stelcos of the world have once again proven. By becoming a member of a firm's board, you can help keep the boardrooms of America honest— and add a plum to your resume at the same time. You'll also make valuable contacts, learn important networking and management skills, and gain a better understanding of what really goes on behind those closed doors.

13 Hire a kid to do your yardwork or fix your computer.

Industrious young people often find it tough to make money—even when they're motivated. Jobs are hard to come by in today's economy, even for those sixteen and older; for younger teens it's even harder. Help ingrain a solid American work ethic in the junior–high schoolers of your choice by hiring them to rake leaves, baby-sit, teach you to use that new software, or create a Second Life avatar for you. You may even learn something yourself.

14 Give a teen a summer job.

Four million teenagers hope to find work each summer—but fewer and fewer are finding it. The competition is fierce, and with the retail, manufacturing, and construction industries suffering slowdowns, there are fewer jobs to compete for. So give a kid a summer job at your workplace or home office, and help the next generation learn to be resourceful, productive, and responsible. Ask your colleagues, friends, and family if they know any teenagers interested in your line of work, and hire them to be your gofer for the summer.

enough!

In 2000, nearly half of all teens aged sixteen to nineteen landed a summer job, but by last summer that number fell to only one third. That's the smallest percentage since the government began documenting teenage work in 1948, according to the Center for Labor Market Studies at Northeastern University.

15 Donate interview clothes to a local women's shelter.

Abused and homeless women trying to make a new start often lack the business attire they need to land that all-important job that will get them get back on their feet. You can recycle your good-enough-to-interview-in suits and dresses by donating them to your local shelter—or you can donate $29 to buy a suit for a woman in need (it's called the Dressing Fine Campaign run by Women in Retail and the Women's Alliance). Just visit *www.thewomens alliance.org* for details.

"Someone's future is hanging in your closet."

— SLOGAN OF THE WOMEN'S ALLIANCE

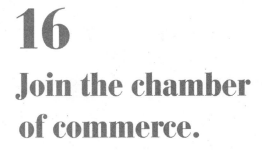
16

Join the chamber of commerce.

17 Invent something.

From squirtguns and exercise equipment to automobile security and laser eye surgery technologies, patents are big business— and big money. Revenues from patent licensing generate some half a trillion dollars every year, according to the U.S. Patent Office. So whether you invent a better mousetrap at home in your basement or on the job at the office, get started.

18 Join SCORE.

Billing itself as "Counselors to America's Small Business," this nonprofit is dedicated to fostering entrepreneurship and small business success nationwide. So share your wisdom and lessons learned in business with the next generation of entrepreneurs—and have fun doing it. Check out *www.score.org* for more information.

19 Pay off all your credit card debt.

If you have massive credit card debt or delinquent accounts, addressing these crisis situations needs to be a top priority. The cost of carrying high-interest debt or allowing delinquencies to affect your credit (FICO) score will defeat your financial goals before you get them off the ground. Once you've fought the debt dragon, you can refocus your goals on savings and wealth creation.

If you vastly reduce your credit card debt and lower the interest rates on the few you maintain, you'll be well on your way to renewed financial solvency—and so will our nation.

"Creditors have better memories than debtors."

— BENJAMIN FRANKLIN

enough!

According to Experian, the average American with a credit file is responsible for $16,635 in debt (not including their mortgages).

Source: *U.S. News and World Report*, "The End of Credit Card Consumerism," August 2008

20 Buy local.

An amazing array of goods, services, and food is available right in your backyard. Rather than driving long distances to shop at monstrous warehouse stores, shop at your local, family-owned grocer or farmers' market. Even if you pay a bit more, when you support local independent businesses, you are improving your local economy. Just as independent bookstores and roadside fruit and vegetable stands are vanishing, so are small, local businesses. Buy local—it's well worth the extra change and it strengthens relationships in your community.

21 Spread the word about your favorite local businesses.

Word of mouth is still the best advertisement. Spread the word amongst your friends and business acquaintances. Is there a locally owned tailor, gift store specializing in handcrafted goods made nearby, sign maker, jeweler, or printer that's not getting enough foot traffic? Be an ambassador for local business, and everyone will thank you for it! And if you own a small business, frequent other local businesses, and give them your business card and ask for referrals. Networking is a *good* thing.

Rallying Cry!

"Academics who followed shoppers found that those in farmers' markets had ten times as many conversations as those in supermarkets."

— BILL MCKIBBEN

Author and activist

enough!

According to the Small Business Administration's Office of Advocacy, unincorporated self-employment dropped from 10.5 million Americans in 2007 to 10.1 million in 2008.

22 Buy American.

Just as trickle-down economics failed to lift the lower and middle classes, so have free market practices failed to improve the American economy. Since the late 1970s, America's desire for cars, foreign oil, and consumer electronics has caused trade deficits that have to be financed by attracting overseas investment. At the end of 2005, the United States had a net debt of $2.7 trillion (source: *Time* magazine). Every time you buy a product that is not made in America, you participate in shipping jobs overseas. Again, if you spend an extra buck for an American product, you are strengthening our economy rather than bolstering those in other nations. Be a patriot in the stores!

THE PRESIDENT SAYS

"I have come to a resolution myself as I hope every good citizen will, never again to purchase any article of foreign manufacture which can be had of American make be the difference of price what it may."

— THOMAS JEFFERSON

23 Repay your student loans.

In the 1970s, college students typically borrowed about 26 percent of the cost; today, college students borrow as much as 80 percent of the cost. Because the federal government funds most student loans, repaying them boosts our federal economy and allows those coming up to have access to an education. Proudly pay down your student loans.

enough!

Some interesting stats on young people in debt:

The average college graduate has nearly $20,000 in debt. Between 1989 and 2004, average credit card debt has increased 47 percent for twenty-five- to thirty-four-year-olds and 11 percent for eighteen- to twenty-four-year-olds. Nearly 20 percent of eighteen- to twenty-four-year-olds are in "debt hardship," up from 12 percent in 1989.

Source: Demos.org, "The Economic State of Young America," May 2008

► Here's how to create a money log:

- List your income.
- List credit card and loan balances, including car loans, student loans, personal loans, mortgages, home equity or line of credit, and any taxes owed.
- List retirement and savings accounts. Including health savings accounts, certificates of deposit (CDs), education accounts, and investments.
- List monthly expenditures, such as utilities, groceries, clothing, automobile gas and upkeep, education expenses, child care expenses, entertainment, and so on.

enough!

According to an American Express Publishing survey, 70 percent of the respondents, all of whom had household discretionary incomes of $100,000 or more, said they preferred to shop online.

24 Keep a money log.

One of the smartest financial tasks you can undertake is to keep track of your money. The first—and very important—task is to discover and record all aspects of your financial situation (see sidebar at left). Stay on top of your daily expenditures by maintaining a money log that records where and how you are really spending your money, modeling the government's new desire for "transparency."

25 Comparison shop online.

Whenever you're looking to buy any non-perishable item, do price comparisons online before buying. Utilize the websites of your preferred stores as well as the websites of online retailers and seek out the best prices. The more expensive the item, the more valuable this comparison shopping can be. You can save 10 to 15 percent off the purchase price of an item (or even more) with just a few moments of research.

26 Reprogram your money mindset.

Try saving your money, not spending it! If you struggle with this revolutionary concept, accentuate the positive. Set healthy financial goals to spend less and accumulate wealth. The point of making goals is to create a positive vision of your future. Instead of writing, "I won't spend money on luxuries for six months," write "I choose to pay down my credit card debt to zero." It's not deprivation; it's empowerment! Before you buy anything, ask yourself if you really need it and if it's worth the price you're paying. Oftentimes, simply pausing before buying will allow you to use greater discretion when spending money.

Rallying Cry!

"A simple rule dictates my buying: Be fearful when others are greedy, and be greedy when others are fearful. And most certainly, fear is now widespread, gripping even seasoned investors."

— WARREN BUFFETT

27 Raise your credit score.

From the obvious (car loans, home mortgages, credit card rates) to the surprising (insurance rates), your credit report has a great deal of influence on the amount you have to pay on almost everything. Even worse, errors on your credit report can cause your rates to go up. Get your credit report for free from the federal government at *www.annualcreditreport.com.*

enough!
On average, at a credit bureau on record, a consumer has thirteen credit obligations, and of these, nine are most likely credit cards and the other four are installment loans.
Source: Myfico.com

28 Pay your bills on time.

Paying your bills on time improves your FICO score, which improves your credit rating, which lowers your interest rates. All of these together make you financially sound and capable of borrowing money to launch a small business, make house repairs, or cover an emergency expense. Paying your bills on time helps your creditors be able to pay their bills on time and to maintain a healthy bottom line.

"If you can count your money, you don't have a billion dollars."

—J. PAUL GETTY

29 Speak up about poor service or workmanship.

Encourage your fellow citizens to elevate their work ethics. By taking pride in our work and the products or services we provide, we support America's reputation for being the best in the world. This concept is not just for major players in the global market, but for every goods or service provider in our country. Whatever you do, do it well. And encourage others to follow suit by nudging them toward taking pride in themselves and their contributions. When you experience disconcerting lapses in quality, write a letter to the CEO or manager and encourage them to motivate their workers to step up and exceed consumer expectations.

▶ As we've learned lately, the economy is circular and interconnected, and it's beneficial to all if we're true to our promises.

30 Negotiate for better terms on your mortgage.

If you have paid down your credit cards and improved your credit score, you may be in an excellent bargaining position to renegotiate for a lower interest rate. If you're paying more than 40 percent of your income for your mortgage, you may be eligible for renegotiation. If your monthly housing cost is around 25 percent, they're not likely to budge, unless your income plummets due to job loss or illness. If you're heading toward foreclosure, however, call your mortgage company immediately and work with them to stay afloat.

"A bank is a place where they lend you an umbrella in fair weather and ask for it back when it begins to rain."

—ROBERT FROST

31 Negotiate for better terms on your credit cards.

Flip your credit card over and call the number on the back. State clearly that you would like the interest rate reduced because it is making it difficult to pay off the card, and that you are considering transferring the balance to another card. If the first person says no, ask to speak to a supervisor. Keep escalating to get a positive answer. Repeat for all your cards. Your finance charges may be greatly reduced, meaning you'll have smaller minimum payments and more breathing room each month.

enough!

Between 1990 and 2000, the total volume of consumer loans—including credit cards, auto loans, and other nonmortgage debt—more than doubled to $1.7 trillion. The average American has around $8,400 in credit card debt.

Source: *www.Bankrate.com*

32 Sign up for automatic payment plans.

This is the best invention since, well, the Internet. Presuming you have enough cash in your bank account when bills come due, arrange to pay your bills automatically. You can often jockey due dates, timing some to arrive early in the month, and others later. Then, create automatic payments for your mortgage, car payments, credit cards, phone, cable, and utilities. Doing so means never being late again! And that frees up your time, bolsters your FICO score, and keeps you on track financially. Here are other benefits of automatic online payments:

★ You receive reminders online.
★ You receive paperless statements.
★ It's easy.
★ Your bills are never late.

► Be sure you have adequate funds on hand! Check your bank balances every week to make sure withdrawals are accurate.

enough!

According to Checkfree corp.com, people pay their debts in the following ways:

21 percent pay on their bank websites
21 pay on the creditor's website
11 percent use automatic online payments
31 percent use checks
2 percent use the telephone (which can be expensive!)
7 percent pay in person

33 Avoid buying new retail products.

Consider buying used or secondhand products or clothing. With the recycling that occurs via eBay these days, you can almost always find what you need by browsing its pages. Other options: Visit local consignment shops and Goodwill outlets, browse on Craigslist.org, or visit *www.freecycle.com.*

34 Establish an emergency fund.

At some point in your life, disaster will strike—and you'll need an emergency fund. Experts recommend that you bank three to eight months of expenses. Even if it seems impossible, start now! Have your bank automatically transfer a small sum out of your checking account each week (say, $20) into a savings account. Make other contributions whenever your budget permits, and keep this account inviolable unless you have a catastrophic emergency.

"Bargaining has neither friends nor relations."

—BENJAMIN FRANKLIN

35 Bargain everywhere for everything.

The Internet is a fabulous educational tool for consumers. An educated consumer is a smart consumer and a financially savvy consumer. Whether you're buying a pair of leather boots or a washing machine, go online and search for information that will help you know a fair price when you're ready to buy. Then, before you buy anything, but particularly big-ticket items, ask your retailer to match the lowest price you've found. These days, more and more retailers bargain. It can't hurt to ask.

haggling tips & tricks

1. Research prices first.
2. Give yourself a price limit, and walk away rather than exceed it.
3. Play up any flaws in the product as bargaining leverage.
4. Pull out what you're willing to pay in cash.
5. Never lose your cool.

Source: *www.howtohaggle.com*

36 Make a budget— and stick to it.

Your primary goal each month should be to spend less than you bring in. To create a workable budget, assemble the following information:

★ *After-tax income:* The amount you receive after your employer withholds income taxes.
★ *Required expenses:* Your unavoidable, necessary costs. Trim where you can, and if you are living beyond your means, lower your expectations, and your spending budget.
★ *Expendable expenses:* Things you may enjoy but don't need to live, such as alcohol, jewelry, expensive groceries, fancy coffees, dining out, movie rentals, or cable/satellite television service.

Subtract your expenses from your income, and if you fall short, prioritize expenses or find a way to make more money. And stick to your budget at all costs! Unlike the federal treasury, you cannot print more money . . . or borrow from China.

"A budget tells us what we can't afford, but it doesn't keep us from buying it."

—WILLIAM FEATHER

SAVE SMARTER

37 Save 10 percent of your salary.

You've undoubtedly heard the adage: Pay yourself first! The more you can increase your savings, the better. Want to know how fast it can add up? Take a look at the following table, and make a commitment to save a mere 10 percent of your monthly salary.

enough!

The Employee Benefit Research Institute found that Americans are not saving: In 2005, the national savings rate was zero. Europeans save 10 percent and Italians 16 percent of their household income.

SAVINGS GIVEN MONTHLY CONTRIBUTIONS					
Years to spending date	$100	$200	$400	$500	$1,000
1	$1,238	$2,476	$4,952	$6,190	$12,380
5	$7,120	$14,239	$28,478	$35,598	$71,196
10	$17,105	$34,210	$68,421	$85,526	$171,052
15	$31,110	$62,221	$124,442	$155,552	$311,105

Switch banks if your bank took bailout money and won't report how it's spending it.

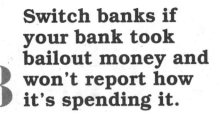

38

Now that the government has handed out major cash—the taxpayer's cash—to bolster banks, keep your own bank accountable. Ask your bank branch for documentation that reveals how their bailout money has been allocated. If they're less than transparent or have misallocated funds, vote with your business—take it elsewhere, to a bank that is acting responsibly.

Rallying Cry!

"The purse of the people is the real seat of sensibility. Let it be drawn upon largely, and they will then listen to truths which could not excite them through any other organ."

— THOMAS JEFFERSON

Switch firms if your investment brokerage firm took bailout money and won't report how it's spending it.

39

Ditto for investment firms. Ask for documentation that proves they are being fiscally responsible and making the best—and intended—use of federal bailout money. Why would you validate their penchant for making bad decisions? Don't support dysfunction! Support the financial firms that are being fiscally responsible and making decisions that bolster our economy—and the oft-mentioned "Main Street."

40 Set up a living trust.

A living trust is a document that assigns a trustee to handle your estate in the event of your death. It's essentially a will that doesn't have to go through probate. You create a list of your beneficiaries, the name of a guardian or guardians, and how you wish matters to be handled. You then draw up a living trust that allows your designated trustee to distribute your estate according to your wishes. This is responsible financial management that protects your family. It also frees up the courts and keeps them out of your personal finances.

enough!

Currently, estates valued at less than $2 million are not subject to federal estate taxes, but this limit fluctuates annually and may revert back to $1 million in 2011. If you are worried about paying extensive state taxes, or you have an estate that's worth more than $2 million, an attorney can help you distribute your assets in ways that minimize taxes.

41 Invest in yourself.

If you're like many Americans, your parents instilled a sense that Americans are innovative and that we can do whatever we set our minds to do. There's no better investment than the one you make in yourself, whether it's furthering your education, launching a small business, or keeping yourself at the top of your game. We—each of us—are America.

"The name of the game is taking care of yourself, because you're going to live long enough to wish you had."

— GRACE MIRABELLA
Former editor-in-chief
of *Vogue*

42 Invest in your community.

As Hillary Clinton so famously titled her book, "It takes a village to raise a child." Every community has a multitude of needs and a shortage of volunteers. Find your niche and use your talents to strengthen your local government, your local community centers, your local sports programs, your local library, or even your city or town council. Our new president eschewed fortune and chose to serve as a community organizer, working with some of Chicago's most disadvantaged and disenfranchised citizens, setting an admirable standard for us all.

43 Invest in your nation.

Too often, we fall under the misconception that America owes us everything we desire. America has been generous to many and to keep America strong, we need to reinvest in our nation. Find your own way, but get participatory. Some ideas:

★ Habitat for Humanity
★ The Peace Corps
★ AmeriCorps
★ Youth sports programs
★ Mentor high school students

▶ **Need more inspiration? Log onto *www.pointsoflight.org* or *www.voa.org* (Volunteers of America).**

44 Neither a borrower nor a lender be.

Living within your means—a tenet our grandparents and parents lived by—has gone out of fashion. Those survivors of the Great Depression were on to something. The advent of credit cards seemed like a good idea—and it's backfired. There are a multitude of reasons to exercise restraint when it comes to borrowing (buying on credit) and lending. The two best ones: The only people truly free are those with no debt; and loaning money to friends and family often weakens relationships. Be fiscally responsible and expect the same of others—and our nation will eventually get on board, including the children who see their parents modeling fiscal responsibility.

"If you would know the value of money, go try to borrow some; for he that goes a-borrowing goes a-sorrowing."

— BENJAMIN FRANKLIN

45 Save all your change and bank it.

You can make this fun. Charge your family a penny, a nickel, a dime, or a quarter for transgressions: not getting their chores done, being late for dinner, not hanging up their towels, or whatever keeps occurring that drives you crazy. Add loose change left lying around, and the piggy bank will fill up. Use a clear plastic piggy bank (or jar) so everyone can enjoy the process. When it's full, make taking it to the bank an outing.

▶ **If you don't have children, look for ways to beef up your savings, like forgoing a manicure and plunking that money into your piggy bank.**

46 Postpone your retirement.

Our 401(k)s have taken a hit, so it's highly likely that many of us will work longer than we planned—and that's not *all* bad. Consider yourself a productive member of our economy and feel good that you will continue to make a contribution. It's all in the attitude. And count your blessings:

★ You'll likely have better healthcare.
★ You'll keep your mind active.
★ We're all in the same boat.
★ Your retirement fund can recoup its losses.

workin' it

A June 2008 Associated Press survey reports that 66 percent of Baby Boomers expect to continue to work after "retiring."

47 Rent out a room to someone who's lost their home.

Why not? If you've got a room to spare, you can help someone who's in a tough spot, and lighten your load. You might even make a new friend. To a person or a family in transition, you could be a lifesaver, and you just might discover the many benefits of sharing your space. Americans are known worldwide for being amazingly generous after catastrophic events, and this financial pinch warrants a little compassion—and a lot of sensibility.

"People first, then money, then things."

—SUZE ORMAN

48 If you're married, try to stay that way.

There are financial advantages to staying married, in addition to the many social and spiritual ones. Stable families create a stable society and a healthier economy. When couples separate, everyone loses—but women *really* lose. Approximately 47 percent of women over the age of fifty are single. Those unmarried female Baby Boomers are expected to live fifteen to twenty years longer than men, but only 20 percent will be financially secure in their retirement. And 58 percent of female Baby Boomers have less than $20,000 saved for retirement.

enough!
When unmarried partners who share a single account break up, all of their money goes to the person who makes the first withdrawal. However, married couples' assets gained during their marriage are usually jointly owned. (Laws vary by state.)
Source: *www.usnews.com*

49 Live with someone and share expenses.

If you're traveling light, renting a room in someone else's house can save you a bundle—and keep your life uncomplicated and flexible. Gone are the days when youngsters moved out of their parents' house, or the dormitory, to live on their own immediately. Most are sharing space, and making the most of it. Some reasons for sharing your living space include paying only half for your cable, Internet, and utility bills, carpooling on errands, having someone to talk to when you come home, and increased security.

"Last night somebody broke into my apartment and replaced everything with exact duplicates. . . . When I pointed it out to my roommate, he said, 'Do I know you?'"

—STEVEN WRIGHT

FIGHT CORPORATE GREED

50 Become a whistleblower.

Don't let corporate greed kill people. In the past, when whistleblowers revealed safety issues regarding products, they often suffered retaliation. Now, thanks to the newly enacted Consumer Product Safety Act of 2008, millions employed in the manufacturing, distribution, and sale of consumer goods are covered by groundbreaking whistleblower protections. The act's sound pro-employee provisions include:

★ The right to a trial by jury
★ Compensatory damages
★ Attorney's fees and costs

So if you are in the position to report a potentially dangerous consumer product, feel safer yourself knowing that this law is now in place.

enough!
According to the U.S. Consumer Product Safety Commission's website, "Deaths, injuries and property damage from consumer product incidents cost the nation more than $800 billion annually."

Rallying Cry!
"Deep Throat did serve the public interest by providing the guidance and information to us . . . his information, and in my view, courage, allowed the newspaper to use what he knew and suspected."

— BOB WOODWARD

51
Boycott companies that outsource jobs overseas.

Outsourcing, offshoring . . . whatever you call it, the loss of American jobs to workers from India, China, and other low-wage nations is growing 20 percent every year, according to outsourcing consultant Michael Corbett. The worst offenders are the multinational corporations, but they're not alone. According to CNN, hundreds of companies are "exporting America"— including Coca-Cola, Anheuser-Busch, Bank of America, AT&T, Apple, Target, Washington Mutual, Thomasville Furniture, Texas Instruments, Nike, Radio Shack, John Deere, Frito Lay, Quaker Oats, and many, many more. See Exporting America at *www .cnn.com* for a full list—and boycott those companies.

52
Outsource to local businesses.

THE PRESIDENT SAYS

"We export only 4,000 cars to Korea; that's not free trade!"

— BARACK OBAMA

Rather than send work overseas, hire local businesses to perform such functions as accounting, payroll, IT, and customer service.

53

Support your local union.

54 Support a minimum wage increase.

Raising the minimum wage was a key promise of the Obama/Biden campaign. From Barack Obama's website:

> Barack Obama and Joe Biden believe that people who work full time should not live in poverty. Even though the minimum wage will rise to $7.25 an hour by 2009, the minimum wage's real purchasing power will still be below what it was in 1968. As president, Obama will further raise the minimum wage to $9.50 an hour by 2011, index it to inflation and increase the Earned Income Tax Credit to make sure that full-time workers can earn a living wage that allows them to raise their families and pay for basic needs such as food, transportation, and housing— things so many people take for granted.

THE PRESIDENT SAYS

"It's time to turn the page for all those Americans who want nothing more than to have a job that can pay the bills and raise a family. Let's finally make the minimum wage a living wage. Let's tie it to the cost of living so we don't have to wait another ten years to see it rise."

— BARACK OBAMA

55 Report egregious corporate policies to a TV station.

Most local TV stations have a reporter dedicated to investigating consumer complaints. Contact yours when you have something to report.

56 Shoot a documentary about local corporate greed.

Watch the Michael Moore classic *Roger & Me* for inspiration. In one scene in his documentary, Moore describes a party after massive layoffs at the GM plant in Flint, Michigan: "The more fortunate in Flint were holding their annual Great Gatsby party at the home of one of GM's founding families. To show that they weren't totally insensitive to the plight of others, they hired local people to be human statues at the party."

57 Write an editorial for your local newspaper.

Have the courage of your convictions. When you see corporate greed run amok in your hometown, tell the offenders and your fellow townspeople what you really think—in print.

"Some of the most far-reaching investigations stem from one single complaint. Telling a journalist what you know can change the lives of others and even overhaul an entire system."

—HANK PHILLIPPI RYAN
Emmy-winning investigative reporter for WHDH-TV in Boston

58 Protest bait-and-switch tactics.

Bait and switch is an underhanded means of drawing you in with a "great deal" and then changing terms on you. When you encounter such tactics (car dealerships and credit card companies are notorious for it!), protest. Ask to speak to the manager and complain. If you receive no satisfaction, follow up with an official letter of complaint to the Better Business Bureau.

THE PRESIDENT SAYS

" . . . America's highest economic need is higher ethical standards, standards enforced by strict laws and upheld by responsible business leaders."

— GEORGE W. BUSH

59 Launch an e-mail campaign against unfair practices.

When you encounter unfair business practices, don't keep it to yourself. Send out an e-mail blast to friends, family, and colleagues, and encourage them to spread the news around. Think of it as viral retribution.

CALL TO Online Action!

Top Five Consumer Websites

www.bbb.org

www.adbusters.org

www.ftc.gov

www.theconsumer activist.com

www.consumer freedom.com

60

If your company spends taxpayer money on parties, etc., refuse to participate.

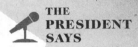

61

If your company spends taxpayer money on parties, etc., alert the media.

Take pictures or shoot video of the goings-on—and drop it off (anonymously if you must) at your local TV station.

62 Boycott companies that offer golden parachutes.

The golden parachute hall of shame:

★ *Henry McKinnell, CEO of Pfizer,* who gave himself a 72 percent raise as the company bled money. Pfizer stock had dropped a whopping 46 percent by the time McKinnell left a year later, pocketing $83 million on the way out the door.

★ *William McGuire, CEO and chairman of UnitedHealth Group Inc.,* who took some $1.6 billion in stock options, often when the company's stock was down, thereby making a killing when they bounced back. McGuire left in 2006 when the government caught on, eventually returning $600 million in payback agreements with the SEC, among others. That left McGuire with "only" $800 million in options.

★ *Charles Prince, CEO of Citigroup Inc.,* who described his resignation during the mortgage crisis as "the only honorable course for me"—taking $99 million in stock and pension benefits with him.

★ *Stanley O'Neal, CEO and chairman of Merrill Lynch & Co. Inc.,* who left in 2007 with $161.5 million just as the company posted the biggest quarterly loss in its ninety-three-year history—$2.3 billion— and was fined $8.4 million for its role in the subprime mortgage crisis.

THE PRESIDENT SAYS

"People would ask me how I could stand the long campaigning, how I could stand being charged with the responsibilities of a great nation, one of the most powerful and difficult jobs in the world. It wasn't any more difficult than picking cotton all day or shaking peanuts."

— JIMMY CARTER

FIGHT GOVERNMENT WASTE

63 Keep an eye out for government waste.

As taxpayers, we all should be on the lookout for government waste—at the local level as well as at the national level. With the deficit at $10.6 trillion and counting, we need to cut the fat wherever we can. Every year, the Citizens Against Government Waste (CAGW) publish the *Congressional Pig Book,* which outlines the pork in the federal budget. The *2008 Pig Book* listed 11,610 pork-barrel line items costing the American taxpayers some $17.2 billion. The most egregious of these are called Oinkers. Some highlights:

The French Kiss-Off Award
Porker: Representative Mike Thompson (D-CA)
Pork: $211,509 for olive fruit fly research in Paris, France

The Tax Dollars on Drugs Award
Porker: Representative John Murtha (D-PA)
Pork: $23 million for the National Drug Intelligence Center

Rallying Cry!

"I blame the lack of regulation more than the leadership. If it was one company, that would be one thing. But it's Bear Stearns, it's Countrywide, it's Lehman Brothers. Now, they were all guilty of drinking the Kool-Aid and buying stuff they shouldn't have bought."

— BARNEY FRANK
Chairman of the House Financial Services Committee, on the Wall Street meltdown

The Pantheon of Pork Award
Porker: Senator Robert Byrd (D-WV)
Pork: A whopping $386 million in pork!

The Narcissist Award
Porker: Representative Charles Rangel (D-NY)
Pork: $1,950,000 for the Charles B. Rangel Center for Public Service

The Pig in Sheep's Clothing Award
Porkers: Montana Senators Max Baucaus (D) and Jon Tester (D)
Pork: $148,950 for the Montana Sheep Institute

The Unidentified Fiscal Object Award
Porker: Representative Ann Esshoo (D-CA)
Pork: $1.6 million for the Allen Telescope Array

The Money Doesn't Grow on Trees Award
Porker: Senator Richard Durbin (D-IL)
Pork: $344,540 for Chicago's GreenStreets Tree Planting Program

The Taxpayers Get Steamed Award
Porker: Maine Senators Susan Collins (R) and Olympia Snowe (R), and Representative Thomas Allen (D-ME)
Pork: $188,000 for the Lobster Institute

---

enough!
The national debt has been rising some *$3.87 billion per day* since September 28, 2007!

THE PRESIDENT SAYS
"When there is a lack of honor in government, the morals of the whole people are poisoned."

— HERBERT HOOVER

---

you're broker than you thought
$10.5 trillion divided by 305,119,408 Americans equals $34,815.23 in debt per person.

64 Alert the media if you encounter government waste.

If CAGW can report Oinkers to the national media, you can report your hometown porkers to your local media.

65 Start an e-mail campaign against instances of government waste.

Launch a viral revolution! Send out an e-mail blast, well, blasting the porkers and pork in your local budget. Encourage your fellow citizens to spread the word as well.

66 Stage a sit-in to protest fiscal irresponsibility at your town hall.

Alert the media, and sit long enough for them to catch your protest on film. Sit longer, and you could be arrested. Your call.

► Sit-ins are back in style. Students have been staging sit-ins on campuses across the land, from the University of Montana to Appalachian State and Penn State. Nine were arrested at UM, thirty-one at Penn State, and six at Appalachian State. According to Montana's Director of University Relations Rita Munzenrider, there hasn't been a similar sit-in at UM since the Vietnam War.

67 Vote against spendthrift budget items at your town hall meetings.

THE PRESIDENT SAYS

"We got plenty of money in Washington. What we need is more priority."

— GEORGE W. BUSH

"A penny saved is not a penny earned if at the end of the day you still owe a quarter."

— MARY LANDRIEU

CALL TO Online Action!

Top Five How-To Blogging Sites
www.problogger.net
www.bloggingtips.com
www.blogsessive.com
http://lorelle.wordpress.com
www.blogospherenews.com

68 Vote for fiscally responsible candidates.

Check their voting records—and make sure you vote for the candidates whose record on pork is clean. There are a number of websites dedicated to providing information on various candidates' voting records. Try *www.votesmart.org*, which lists the voting records of current candidates and officials by state.

69 Write an editorial for your local newspaper.

An impassioned argument against spend-thrift politicians and the waste of taxpayers' money is a call to action. You can sound that call within your community by writing an editorial for your local newspaper.

70 Blog about wasteful spending.

Move over, Arianna Huffington, there's a new blog in town. Start your own blog, and pepper it with pork-busting commentary. Invite your fellow citizens to post as well.

71

Note instances of government waste and post them online.

There are a variety of websites where you can report instances of government waste. Whether you're a liberal or a conservative, a Libertarian or a Green, you can find an empathetic place to tell your story:

www.cagw.org
www.huffingtonpost.com
http://porkreport.blogivists.com
www.townhall.com
www.theoinkreport.com

THE PRESIDENT SAYS

"Sure, there are dishonest men in local government. But there are dishonest men in national government, too."

— RICHARD M. NIXON

72

Contact a local TV reporter if you encounter wasteful government spending.

Most local TV stations have a political journalist who's always on the lookout for stories of local pork. In a post–Bridge-to-Nowhere world, taxpayers will be sensitive to even the faintest whiff of pork. These stories will continue to attract viewers— and the reporters know it. So give 'em a leg up.

"Greed is good."

— MICHAEL DOUGLAS

As Gordon Gekko in the Oliver Stone film *Wall Street*

THE PRESIDENT SAYS

"Here is my principle: Taxes shall be levied according to ability to pay. That is the only American principle."

— FRANKLIN D. ROOSEVELT

73 Sign a petition for waste-cutting propositions.

Every election, measures and propositions designed to curb government spending appear on ballots across America. You can be part of the effort to propose and enact measures by signing the petitions required to put the measure on the ballot. So put your John Hancock where it counts.

"There, I guess King George will be able to read that."

— JOHN HANCOCK

On signing the Declaration of Independence

74 Support legislation to regulate Wall Street.

In the wake of the recent Wall Street melt-down, politicians and taxpayers are clamoring for a solution. Deregulation got us into this mess; regulation can help get us out.

THE PRESIDENT SAYS

"I believe that banking institutions are more dangerous to our liberties than standing armies."

— THOMAS JEFFERSON

75 Support legislation to regulate the banking industry, too.

PART
TWO

KEEP
AMERICA
GREEN

CHAPTER 6

GREEN YOUR WORK

55

76.

Use public transportation.

55

77.

Drive a hybrid.

56

78.

Bike to work.

56

79.

Start a carpool.

57

80.

Plant a tree every time you fly.

58

81.

Telecommute.

58

82.

Hire a telecommuter.

59

83.

Cut down on disposable products.

60

84.

Reuse or donate old office equipment.

61

85.

Recycle office items.

62

86.

Think less ink.

63

87.

Start a recycling co-op with other small businesses.

63

88.

Go paperless.

64

89.

Correspond via e-mail rather than snail mail.

65

90. Use online videoconferencing. 66	**91.** Make your product or service more green. 66	**CHAPTER 7** **GREEN YOUR HOME** 67
92. Reduce, reuse, recycle—*really!* 67	**93.** Use online video chat at home. 69	**94.** Go solar. 69
95. Replace all your incandescent lightbulbs. 70	**96.** Swap out your conventional water heater for a tankless one. 70	**97.** Use the short cycles when you run a dishwasher. 71
98. Use surge protector strips and turn them off at night. 71	**99.** Teach your kids to turn the lights off. 72	**100.** Turn the thermostat down—and bundle up. 73
101. Turn the ceiling fan on to keep warm. 74	**102.** Build your own windmill. 74	**103.** Clean green. 75

104.

Go meatless twice a week.

76

105.

Join WE.

77

106.

Teach your kids not to litter.

77

107.

Watch your water consumption.

78

CHAPTER 8

GROW YOUR GARDENS GREEN

79

108.

Grow a community garden.

79

109.

Volunteer to help clean up a local place.

80

110.

Support your local green spaces.

80

111.

Put in desert landscaping.

81

112.

Stop using pesticides.

81

113.

Start a compost pile.

82

114.

Support your local produce group initiative.

83

115.

Shop at local farms and organic markets.

83

116.

Grow native plants.

84

117.

Adopt an acre of wetlands.

84

118.

Organize an Earth Day cleanup.

85

119.

Support alternative energy sources.

87

120.

Document illegal dumping.

88

121.

Alert the media to local environmental issues.

89

122.

Report environmental hazards to the EPA.

89

123.

Protest developers threatening green spaces.

90

124.

Spearhead a boycott of a business known for polluting the environment.

90

125.

Write letters to your elected officials.

91

126.

Identify any local environmental hazard—and fight it.

91

127.

Live in an environmentally conscious city.

92

128.

Live in an Energy Star State.

93

129.

Vote for green-minded candidates.

93

130.

Run for office yourself on a green platform.

94

GREEN YOUR WORK

76 Use public transportation.

Mass transit helps reduce the number of cars on the road. Numbers vary, but the Maryland Department of Transportation estimates that a full bus eliminates sixty cars from the road and that translates to reduced vehicle emissions. Find out more about the bus service in your area by contacting your local transit authority or by looking online for schedules and routes. Taking the bus allows riders time to read, listen to music, and even catch up on sleep on the way to work or school. Bus rides can also be substitutes for long car trips. Greyhound and Trailways buses travel across the country, allowing riders to check out vistas along the way. Before making a trip, ask about meal stops and consider bringing along a pillow and snacks to make the trip more enjoyable.

by the numbers

According to the American Public Transportation Association's *2008 Publication Transportation Fact Book*, buses represent 54 percent of the 155,000 public transportation vehicles in active service. Other modes of public travel are paratransit vehicles, heavy rail cars, commuter rail cars, and light rail cars.

77 Drive a hybrid.

Hybrids, when compared to their gasoline-powered counterparts, get about 20 to 35 percent better gas mileage, and they produce fewer emissions than cars that run strictly on gasoline. Check out *www.fueleconomy.gov*, run by the U.S. Department of Energy and the Environmental Protection Agency, to compare and view emissions statistics. The price of a hybrid is higher partly because it also includes the cost of developing new technology—and that's good for America.

"Now that President Bush doesn't run anymore, he rides his mountain bike fanatically. People wonder why he stays at the ranch so long, it might be the mountain bike trails."

—LANCE ARMSTRONG

78 Bike to work.

The city of Davis, California, boasts more bicycles than cars with its wide streets and network of bike paths. Davis's mild climate encourages bike travel, which the city estimates makes up 20 to 25 percent of all trips. Legislation like the national Bicycle Commuter Act, introduced in 2005, encourages employers to support bicycle commuting by offering tax incentives. The costs of bike commuting, such as lights and bike repair, are also covered. If you choose to bike, familiarize yourself with local laws and be careful when sharing the road with cars.

79 Start a carpool.

If you live in an area where riding mass transit isn't feasible but you still want to take a car or two off the road, consider carpooling. A number of websites match destinations and drivers looking to save money and vehicle use. Check out sites like:

www.erideshare.com
www.carpoolconnect.com
www.icarpool.com
www.rideshareonline.com

Ridesharing offers companionship and a break from always having to be behind the wheel, plus many states have carpool lanes. These lanes allow high-occupancy vehicles to sidestep traffic for a less congested ride.

Car sharing has increased as well, and you'll find a variety of programs available. Businesses such as Zipcar (*www.zipcar.com*) and Flexcar (*www.flexcar.com*) operate in numerous cities across the United States, including New York, Chicago, and Los Angeles. Cooperatives like City Carshare (*www.citycarshare.org*) in San Francisco operate as nonprofits.

slow down!

According to the U.S. Department of Energy, for every 5 miles an hour you drive over 60 mph, it's like spending an extra twenty cents per gallon of gas.

Rallying Cry!

"Carpooling is slightly inconvenient, but it saves tremendously on transportation costs and fuel prices."

— ED RENDELL
Governor of Pennsylvania

80 Plant a tree every time you fly.

The new growth will help offset the pollution caused by your flight. To plant your own tree, go to *www.treepeople.org* for information on how to plant it. You can plant trees for other occasions too, of course. For $35, Friends of Trees will plant a young native tree in honor or memory of a friend or loved one and send a card to the person you designate acknowledging your gift. For $100, they will plant a grove of six young native trees.

81 Telecommute.

Now that we're wired for the twenty-first century, telecommuting is more viable. If the work you do doesn't require being onsite, lobby your boss for the chance to telecommute. If he or she is hesitant, start out by asking for a trial period of two days a week, and offer to re-evaluate after three months. The savings could be monumental. You'll save on gas, time, wardrobe, and wear-and-tear (on your car and you!). Your boss could save on office space and telephone and electric bills. Come up with a list of reasons why it benefits your boss, and you may be working in your bathrobe in no time.

82 Hire a telecommuter.

If you're an employer, hiring telecommuters to perform jobs that don't require them to be onsite can have a multitude of positive benefits—for your bottom line and the environment. Some companies are set up for telecommuting, using field representatives or contractors who work out of their houses. Many others can learn to creatively adopt—and adapt to—telecommuting.

According to the Society for Human Resources Management's 2007 Benefits Survey, in 2007, 33 percent of companies offered telecommuting programs to part-time employees, 48 percent to ad hoc employees, and 21 percent to full-time employees.

Besides cutting back on gas emissions and energy excess, benefits of working from home are many, including decreasing the cost and environmental impact from dry cleaning.

"There's a sense that people who telecommute are more flexible. They can combine their home and work life, and they will go the extra yard when needed because they've been given the opportunity to better manage their time."

— DANA GARDNER

Interarbor Solutions
Principal Analyst

Source: *www.eCommerceTimes.com*

83 Cut down on disposable products.

Here are common ways to reduce waste in the office:

★ Reduce paper. Encourage employees to work and communicate electronically. Make double-sided copies for handouts at meetings to conserve paper.

★ Choose your printer inks and toners carefully. Reuse and refill toners; recycle ink cartridges.

★ Reuse office equipment. If you upgrade your computer system, you may be left with fully functioning machines that still have a lot of life in them. Donate them to charities or give them back to your supplier instead of throwing them away.

★ Prepare ahead. If your business has a kitchen, cafeteria, or coffee machine, encourage employees to bring their own mugs and silverware.

★ Reuse boxes and other shipping and packaging materials.

★ Reuse old envelopes for interoffice mail.

"Let every individual and institution now think and act as a responsible trustee of Earth."

—JOHN MCCONNELL

Founder of International Earth Day

84 Reuse or donate old office equipment.

E-waste includes cell phones, computers, televisions, VCRs, copiers, and fax machines—anything with a battery or a plug. While some of this equipment can be recycled or donated to charities, much of it is obsolete or broken. When taken to a landfill for disposal, e-waste takes up valuable room—and it releases metals such as mercury and lead into the environment (although placing e-waste in a landfill is healthier for the environment than incineration—when incinerated, the plastics release dioxins into the air).

The only national legislation regarding e-waste applies to cathode ray tubes (CRT) from computer and television monitors. This legislation states that CRT will not be considered solid waste when processed for recycling. This act saves recyclers from having to abide by strict solid waste regulations and keeps the waste from being considered hazardous. But because it only affects one component of the volume of e-waste generated, it doesn't really help the e-waste recycling industry as a whole.

enough!

According to Eiae.org, the original owner of a laptop, on average, keeps it for three years, and the average user discards a cell phone after two years. However, these electronic devices and others can still be used by schools and charities. Some electronics stores will take your old materials for recycling. Call local stores to find out whether they will allow you to drop off your old electronics for recycling.

85 Recycle office items.

Some common office items that can be recycled include:

★ Aluminum cans
★ Batteries (better yet, use rechargeable batteries)
★ Cardboard boxes
★ Computers
★ Glass
★ Ink cartridges
★ Magazines
★ Paper
★ Plastics

"I only feel angry when I see waste. When I see people throwing away things we could use."

— MOTHER TERESA

Talk to your boss and coworkers about establishing a recycling program in the office. As it gets off the ground, share the problems and successes experienced. Share the quantities of recycling being performed along with any revenue generated. Consider donating the revenue to an employee program, such as a scholarship, or to a local charity.

For locations of recycling organizations, visit *www.earth911.org*.

86 Think less ink.

Ink cartridges can be costly, but there are a number of ways to reduce the use of ink. When printing a document that is not final, print it in draft mode. The draft mode on your printer uses approximately 50 percent less ink than normal print mode. You can also buy software that allows more control over the amount of ink a printer uses. Although using the software may not save as much ink as printing in draft mode, it does offer some in-between options.

enough!
In America, according to Planetgreenrecycle.com, cartridge recycling saves more than 40,000 tons of plastic and metal from landfills annually. In addition, 100,000 used cartridges that are recycled save 1,000,000 liters of oil, 9,599 kilograms of aluminum, and 40 tons of plastic.

87 Start a recycling co-op with other small businesses.

If your office does not generate a lot of one particular kind of recyclable, it might work best to combine efforts with other offices in the area. Look into participating in a cooperative that could get better prices in purchasing recycling equipment and might be the difference between paying to have your recyclables picked up and making money from them. Smaller haulers may also be available at better rates than larger haulers for taking away materials.

► If your business is located in a rural area, you may not be able to join a co-op or a use mom-and-pop hauler. In this case, try second-hand hauling. When office supplies or other items are delivered to the office, the hauler may be able to pick up your recyclables and take them to a recycling facility for you.

88 Go paperless.

Since the onset of personal computers, the amount of paper generated has sky-rocketed. Not only is paper a waste product, it's expensive and diminishes natural resources. Rally your coworkers and come up with milestone goals for the percentage reduction in paper used.

Printing documents is the main paper drain. Think first before printing and make sure all documents are spell-checked and formatted correctly so they don't have to be printed again. When making copies, double-side the documents. If you are producing handouts for a meeting, consider whether they are necessary. Other ways to cut back while maintaining a professional appearance include minimizing margins, decreasing font size, and eliminating double-spacing. These changes will add up over time, especially when printing large documents.

Beyond printing, look for other paper-based tasks that could be done onscreen or online. Office supplies can be ordered online, conference or training requests submitted via electronic form, and even timesheets and expense reports can be completed online. This saves time, eliminating the need to shuttle paper from one desk to another, and it saves resources, too.

► By reducing the amount of paper used in the office, you can reduce the amount of paper your company needs to purchase, store, and deliver.

enough!

According to the Michigan Department of Environmental Quality, the ordinary business office produces around 1.5 pounds of paper waste per employee each day.

89 Correspond via e-mail rather than snail mail.

E-mailing saves paper and the cost of postage. These days, many businesses rely almost solely on e-mail and electronic file sharing—even publishers! Here are five advantages of using e-mail:

1. *It's easy!* You can manage all your correspondence onscreen and so can your customers. Your proposal can be answered, revised, stored, and sent to others, all without reams of paper involved.
2. *It's fast!* Mail is delivered instantly from your office to anywhere in the world. Decisions can be made in a heartbeat.
3. *It's cheap!* Compared to telephone calls, faxes, or overnight courier service, e-mail is a bargain.
4. *It's efficient!* The reader can identify correspondence that needs to be handled immediately, and stash others in a folder to address later. You can also receive voice-mails via e-mail, saving the time it takes to listen to long messages.
5. *It's safe!* Not only is it private, unlike telephone messages or faxes, the industry continually focuses on improving already tight security levels. They typically reach the person more directly than other ways of relaying messages.

enough!

According to *USA Today*, in February 2008, the top four e-mail providers were:

1. Microsoft, with 256.2 million users
2. Yahoo, with 254.6 million users
3. Google, with 91.6 million users
4. AOL, with 48.9 million users

90 Use online videoconferencing.

Online videoconferencing can save on travel expenses. Since the technology has made leaps and bounds and is very low cost, there's every reason to keep up with the times and use Skype or other videoconferencing services as often as possible to conduct your long-distance meetings.

91 Make your product or service more green.

▶ Pacific Natural Foods—an Oregon-based company whose product line includes soups, broths, beverages, and ready-made meals—shows its commitment to environmental responsibility in its procurement and packaging efforts. The company tries to get its ingredients from local farms to reduce the amount of fossil fuels required to ship the food, and it works diligently with manufacturers to reduce waste and design the most efficient and environmentally friendly packaging.

Sustainable, or green, businesses operate in ways that improve or minimize their damage to the environment. These companies work to integrate economic, environmental, and social considerations into the business network. Changes to business practices may have impacts as far-reaching as those of the Industrial Revolution. Get on board and create your own green revolution. Look for ways to adopt green technology and green practices in the way you do business, and in what you create or provide.

GREEN YOUR HOME

92 Reduce, reuse, recycle—*really!*

Until manufacturing has conquered the obstacles to successful sustainability, it's up to consumers to make educated decisions about how to reduce consumption when purchasing products. Follow these general rules:

1. *Make a list.* Whether you're shopping for groceries, school supplies, makeup, or home repair items, sticking with a list will avoid unnecessary or impulse purchases.
2. *Avoid the just-in-case purchase.* If you aren't sure you need something, assume you don't. Being organized at home can help you know what you have in stock.
3. *Evaluate want versus need.* Consider if a purchase is for something you need or want. If it's just a desire, can it be nixed?

THE PRESIDENT SAYS

"Solid wastes are the discarded leftovers of our advanced consumer society. This growing mountain of garbage and trash represents not only an attitude of indifference toward valuable natural resources, but also a serious economic and public health problem."

— JIMMY CARTER

4. *Beware of bargains.* They're designed to move merchandise, not necessarily to save you money.

5. *Beware of warehouses.* That twenty-five-pound bag of flour may seem like a good deal, but if it ends up getting thrown away, it's not.

6. *Walk to the store.* You'll buy only what you can comfortably carry.

Reuse materials by taking small steps that can be incorporated into your life a little at a time. Here are a few for starters:

1. *Reuse totes and bags.* When going to the store, take along your own bags. Some stores even give you small discounts for doing so.

2. *Make a charitable donation.* If you know of an organization in your area that's looking for household items, clothes, or even cell phones, consider making a donation.

3. *Be creative.* Reuse printed-on paper as scrap paper. Packaging materials can be used for craft projects. Sunday comics make colorful wrapping paper.

It is simple to recycle at home. Keep the recycling containers in a convenient location. Eventually recycling will become a habit that you incorporate into everyday tasks. Separating the recyclables is one of the most important factors when it comes to making recycling economical.

▶ **The recycling loop includes three steps: collecting recyclable materials, physically recycling the materials, and purchasing items made from recycled materials.**

"Thank God men cannot fly, and lay waste the sky as well as the earth."

— HENRY DAVID THOREAU

93 Use online video chat at home.

Many of us have friends and acquaintances living in another part of the United States, or even another part of the world. Before driving or flying to visit them, consider conducting video chats using Skype or another such service to catch up on news. You'll keep in touch *and* save on emissions!

94 Go solar.

Solar energy is produced when the sun shines on photovoltaic (PV) panels. These panels hold semiconductors that use the sunlight to generate direct current (DC) electricity. Panels are rated in watts, based on the amount of electricity they can produce under ideal sun and temperature conditions. Customers can choose panels based on their personal electric demands. Panels are usually mounted on the roof, on steel poles, or on the ground. Visit the website *www.findsolar.com* if you are considering installing a home solar system. Beyond explaining monetary savings, the website also calculates the amount of greenhouse gas, in carbon dioxide equivalents, that you'll save.

"It wasn't the Exxon Valdez captain's driving that caused the Alaskan oil spill. It was yours."

— GREENPEACE ADVERTISEMENT

New York Times, 25 February 1990

enough!

In 2007, the United States had nearly 150 megawatts of solar capacity come "online" for a total of 750 megawatts, an increase of 45 percent from the prior year.

Source: Reuters

▶ Compact fluorescent lights (CFLs) are a little more expensive than incandescent bulbs, but they make up for it in longevity and reduced energy use. Over the span of 10,000 hours, a CFL can cost less than half as much energy as an incandescent.

95 Replace all your incandescent lightbulbs.

Did you know that an incandescent lightbulb wastes upward of 95 percent of the energy as heat? This means that the lights are only about 5 percent efficient. And halogen lights do not fare much better, at only 9 percent efficiency. At 20 percent efficiency, compact fluorescent lights (CFLs) are four times more efficient than incandescent lights. To start, simply replace the five lights most frequently used in your home. These lights are most likely in the kitchen, dining room, living room, over the bathroom vanity, and on the front porch.

insulate your water heater

Many modern water heaters are already well insulated, but not all are, and even a well-insulated heater can use a little extra help. The Iowa Energy Center reports that a properly installed insulation blanket can reduce energy loss by 25 to 45 percent on a water heater. If you lose even a dollar's worth of energy from your water heater, the blanket will pay for itself in just a few years (and it's likely that you lose even more energy than that). Go to your local hardware store and ask about a water heater blanket.

96

Swap out your conventional water heater for a tankless one.

97 Use the short cycles when you run a dishwasher.

Researchers at the University of Bonn in Germany determined that using a dishwasher (rather than washing by hand) cleaned the dishes better and saved energy and time. But, you can conserve energy by using the shortest cycles for your dishwasher and washing machine. You can also reduce other environmental impacts when doing the laundry by washing clothes in cold water to save energy and using the smallest amount of soap or detergent.

enough!

The average showerhead uses 2.6 gallons of water per minute, and water costs about $1.50 per 1,000 gallons used. Every time you dawdle in your daily shower and use five minutes' worth of extra water flow, you waste 4,745 gallons of water each year. That adds up to about $7.50 in lost water for time just spent dawdling when you could be doing something else.

98 Use surge protector strips and turn them off at night.

Many home electronic devices continue to use electricity even when turned off. It's often called the "phantom load," and is commonly found in electronics like cell phone chargers, laptop chargers, and small home electric devices and appliances. However, you can put many of your devices on a single surge protector, and then plug that device into an outlet in your home powered by a switch. When you're done with the equipment, flip the switch for instant energy savings. You can even get a remote-controlled surge protector that will provide much the same functionality.

▶ Some devices can consume as much as 40 watts in standby mode, which costs you a dime a day at current energy costs. Though a dime may not seem like a lot, imagine if all Americans fixed this problem in their own homes? That'd be a lot of money and energy saved.

99 Teach your kids to turn the lights off.

Being a parent is a great opportunity to set a good example for future generations. What children learn growing up will stay with them the rest of their lives. Trying to lead a greener family life doesn't have to happen overnight. Parents, tackle items or concerns one by one, and then get ready to improvise. Begin with measures you can easily take, like turning off the lights!

A typical incandescent bulb uses 60 or 75 watts. That means that every fifteen hours or so, it consumes a kilowatt-hour of energy, costing you a dime at current average energy rates. Going through your home to turn off lights before you leave, or even flipping off switches as you wander through your home, can save significant money over the long haul. Got a strip of lights in your bathroom eating 60 watts each? Leaving them on for just a few hours eats a dime, and flipping off that switch before you leave for work can save you thirty cents or so. A minute's worth of walking through your house to turn off lights can be an extremely cost-effective use of your time.

"I think the environment should be put in the category of our national security. Defense of our resources is just as important as defense abroad. Otherwise what is there to defend?"

— ROBERT REDFORD

100 Turn the thermostat down— and bundle up.

Turn your thermostat down ten degrees at night and up again in the morning, unless no one is going to be home during the day. To keep warm, if you live primarily in one room—the family room—turn the heat down throughout the house and use small space heaters to warm that small space. Also, layer clothing, wearing undershirts, sweaters, wool socks or slippers, scarves around your neck, even knit hats indoors (if you tend to freeze), and lay blankets over your lap while watching T.V or reading. Other ways to conserve energy include:

★ Plug up any areas where air seeps out in winter with weatherstripping.
★ Use the sun as an ally. In winter open your drapes to let the sunlight in during the day, and close them at night.
★ Avoid fluctuations in temperature. Of course it's good to lower your thermostat at night, but moving the regulator up and down erratically can increase energy costs.

If you know what your "standard" temperature is, raise it up four degrees in the summer and lower it by four degrees in the winter. This will significantly reduce the effort put forth by your heating and cooling appliances and save you energy money over the long run.

"We do not inherit the earth from our ancestors, we borrow it from our children."

—NATIVE AMERICAN PROVERB

enough!

According to Alliant Energy PowerHouse, if you use a programmable thermostat that lowers the temperature in your house by ten degrees over an eight-hour period, you can reduce your heating costs by 10 percent.

101

Turn the ceiling fan on to keep warm.

Believe it or not, a simple ceiling fan can help reduce your home's energy consumption by pushing warm air down (when it's cold out) by twirling one way, and bringing warm air up (when it's hot out) by twirling the other way. So shut off that energy-hogging AC and enjoy the soft breeze instead. When you do need your AC, be sure to maintain your current model by cleaning filters, checking ducts for leaks, and installing programmable thermostats to adjust the times the house is heated and cooled throughout the day. Also, consider installing a whole-house fan that pulls cool air in and releases warm air through the attic.

enough!

Air circulation can make the room feel as much as 8 degrees cooler, and combined with a temperature-adjustment strategy it can save you as much as 30 percent on your cooling bill.

102

Build your own windmill.

Wind can provide the means of powering your house. Maps indicating wind energy potential for the country are available (at *www.windpoweringamerica.gov*) to determine if your home is located within an area where wind power would be effective. When choosing a location for a wind turbine, take topography and terrain into account, and consider your local wildlife. Research can minimize negative impacts while providing renewable energy to your home.

(not) enough!

According to the American Wind Energy Association, in January 2005, the United States had installed about 6,740 megawatts of wind power capacity, which generates over 17 billion kilowatt-hours annually. That is enough electricity for around 4.3 million people to use each year. It's good, but not enough!

103 Clean green.

People cleaned their houses long before fancy products hit the market and commercials hit the airwaves. In many cases, the "old school," environmentally friendly cleaning ingredients are less expensive than the new and improved products being advertised. When picking out cleansers for the home, try to avoid unnecessary dyes and fragrances and extra packaging. Be careful with concentrates. Using a cleanser that comes in concentrated form does save on packaging by allowing consumers to mix it up and dilute it at home. But in its concentrated form, you must avoid exposing people and the environment from the highly concentrated ingredients.

Here's a list of more natural and less toxic cleaning ingredients and their uses:

★ Vinegar can be mixed with water to clean floors.
★ Borax mixed with lemon juice can be used to clean toilets.
★ Lemon juice mixed with olive oil is great for polishing furniture.
★ Use rubbing alcohol mixed with vinegar and water to clean your windows.
★ Baking soda can be used to scrub stainless steel, iron, or copper pots. Be sure *not* to use it on aluminum pots.

enough!
According to the Consumer Product Safety Commission (CPSC), every year, roughly 150,000 Americans are treated in emergency rooms for injuries related to household chemicals.

104 Go meatless twice a week.

Vegetarianism—a lifestyle based on a choice not to consume meat, fish, or poultry—has been practiced for thousands of years. The choice can be based on health, religion, or personal preference, but the well-being of the environment has become another reason to embrace vegetarianism in recent years. Being a vegetarian does not automatically exclude dairy products or eggs from the diet; that's an individual choice.

Vegans practice a stricter form of vegetarianism. They eat no animal flesh or products and abstain from wearing or using animal products such as leather, silk, wool, lanolin, or gelatin. Then there are dietary vegans who adhere to a strict diet but are amenable to using animal products.

But you don't have to go radical; how about going meatless for two days a week? It will benefit the planet—and your waistline!

"I have no doubt that it is a part of the destiny of the human race, in its gradual improvement, to leave off eating animals."

— HENRY DAVID THOREAU

105 Join WE.

The WE Campaign is a project of the Alliance for Climate Protection, a nonprofit, nonpartisan effort founded by Nobel laureate and former vice president Al Gore. The goal is to build a movement that creates the political will to solve the climate crisis, including a focus on getting America to receive 100 percent of its electricity from clean energy sources within ten years. According the WE website, making this switch will generate millions of good American jobs, cut energy costs, safeguard national security, and protect the climate. We need business and government leaders at all levels to help adopt policies and practices now that will enable America to switch to energy sources with zero carbon emissions. Join WE in lobbying for policies that encourage energy efficiency, renewable energy, and a unified national electricity grid. Check them out on *www.wecansolveit.org*.

Rallying Cry!

"We must now lift our nation to reach another goal that will change history. Our entire civilization depends upon us now embarking on a new journey of exploration and discovery. Our success depends on our willingness as a people to undertake this journey and to complete it within ten years. Once again, we have an opportunity to take a giant leap for humankind."

— AL GORE

106

Teach your kids not to litter.

"Take your life in your own hands, and what happens? A terrible thing: no one to blame."

— ERICA JONG

107

Watch your water consumption.

Beyond taking shorter and cooler showers, consider taking other steps to conserve water and natural resources. Standard showerheads put out up to 5 gallons per minute (gpm). Low-flow showerheads can cut that in half. If a low-flow shower isn't satisfactory, try using an aerator shower-head. Air is added to the water as it flows from the head, making it feel like a higher flowing showerhead. You can also add aerators to spigots, reducing a flow of more than 2 gpm to about 1 gpm. Aerators are relatively inexpensive and easy to install. About one-quarter of the water used in an average home goes to flushing the toilet if efficient toilets aren't installed. Homes built before 1992 that haven't been updated, probably use 3.6 gallons per flush (gpf) model toilets. Newer models use only 1.5 gallons per flush. This reduces the amount of water being pumped from aquifers and streams, treated, and piped to the house, and also saves on treating and discharging the used water, too.

enough!

According to the Alternative Energy Institute (AEI), while more than half the population of the world lives individually on 25 gallons per a day, the average U.S. citizen's daily consumption of water is 159 gallons.

"There are no passengers on Spaceship Earth. We are all crew."

— MARSHALL MCLUHAN

GROW YOUR GARDENS GREEN

108 Grow a community garden.

Gather and inspire neighbors and other members of your community to come together to plant a beautiful and eco-friendly garden that will benefit your community—and the environment. You can invite everyone, including children right up through expert gardeners, to participate. The only qualification will be a willingness to join together and to have fun, while doing something positive. Local garden clubs are likely to offer advice and even cuttings. So roll up your pantlegs and get digging. Hint: Basil, chives, marigolds, chrysanthemums, and mint will repel insects—naturally—so put plenty in the mix and avoid pesticides!

THE PRESIDENT SAYS

"Food is not a commodity like others. We should go back to a policy of maximum food self-sufficiency. It is crazy for us to think we can develop countries around the world without increasing their ability to feed themselves."

— BILL CLINTON

109 Volunteer to help clean up a local place.

Help preserve your surroundings by organizing friends and neighbors to spend an occasional Saturday or Sunday afternoon working together in teams to pick up litter, clear away brush, and beautify the bounteous gifts of nature around you in parks, on ponds, or in woods. Local clubs, children's clubs, and hiking or sporting clubs might be just the ticket for ferreting out volunteers. Think local when it comes to beautifying and think globally when it comes to attracting enthusiasts for your projects.

► Watch your local papers for any community meetings, town council meetings, or city council meetings that involve green spaces in your community. Read up on the issues and go prepared to state your piece and sway others to care as deeply as you do about protecting and preserving green space.

110 Support your local green spaces.

One thing leads to another, and once you plant a community garden and clean up your surroundings, supporting your local green places gets in your blood. You could have a "Tree Huggers" party and invite everyone to purchase a tree to plant, and round up neighbors to contribute environmentally friendly bushes and shrubs or flowering plants. Seasonal events could incorporate themes, such as "spring-clean your community green."

111 Put in desert landscaping.

In the southern and southwestern United States, xeriscape landscaping has become a popular alternative to high-maintenance yards. Xeriscaping uses plants specifically selected for their drought-resistant qualities. Also, wildflowers and short grasses, such as ryegrass, clover, daisies, lavender, and thyme will flourish with little care. Ask your local florist or garden center for products or look some up online.

"I am the Lorax, I speak for the trees, for the trees have no tongues."

— DR. SEUSS

lucky leaf

Clover is marvelously drought-resistant, tolerant to weeds and insects, requires minimal mowing, and offers a soft cushion for walking. So plant clover and spend your weekends looking for lucky four-leaf clovers!

112 Stop using pesticides.

The overuse of pesticides has been acknowledged, and individuals, corporations, and municipalities have begun to use more safety precautions. The EPA registers pesticides for use on the basis that they do not pose unreasonable risks to people or the environment. Unfortunately, the long-term and synergistic effects are not always known when the chemicals are registered. By following the rules for a smart home and yard that are listed here, you should not have to use many pesticides. But if you do, be smart about it and research what you're doing to your lawn, family, and world before you spray chemicals into the air.

▶ To repel pests, mix a few tablespoons of cayenne, garlic, or horseradish with a quart of water and spray it on plants. Recipes for mildew and fungi treatments include common kitchen ingredients like baking soda and vinegar—do an online search to find these.

113 Start a compost pile.

One way to pump up plants and get rid of garbage at the same time is to compost. Compost is made of recycled food scraps, yard trimmings, clean paper, and even fireplace ashes. Don't include meat, pet droppings, or oil and grease though because they can attract rodents that can carry disease and can kill the beneficial organisms. You can buy a compost unit from lawn and garden centers, online carriers, or even through local extension or utility offices. Or you can make one at home using materials such as chicken wire, bricks, or buckets. The organic material in the compost bin needs to be turned and watered regularly to mix up the contents from the inner portions of the pile to the outer portions. The material in the center of the pile decays as it is kept warm and moist, a perfect atmosphere for degradation. When the mixture turns into a dark brown, crumbly material that smells like earth it's ready to go. Using compost is a great way to improve soil texture and keep weeds from growing; it increases air and water absorption in the soil, and can be used as mulch in the lawn or garden. Compost makes great potting soil.

enough!

According to the Environmental Protection Agency (EPA) up to 31 million tons of yard waste is collected, transported, and processed by municipalities every year. If raking isn't possible, consider manual leaf sweepers to collect leaves from yards, sidewalks, and driveways, making them ready to put in the compost pile (*www.composters.com*).

114 Support your local produce group initiative.

Local and family farms are quickly becoming a thing of the past. Support them by buying locally grown produce and by donating to Farm Aid (*www.farmaid.org*). Get together with your friends for a day of fruit picking from local orchards. When you've plucked all the bounty from the trees, take a few boxes or bags of the fruit to a local food bank or homeless shelter. Plant an apple tree, just like Johnny Appleseed—apples are symbols of love.

THE PRESIDENT SAYS

"Farming looks mighty easy when your plow is a pencil and you're a thousand miles from the corn field."

— DWIGHT D. EISENHOWER

115 Shop at local farms and organic markets.

In order to have a variety of fruits and vegetables available year-round they have to be transported. This increases the consumption of fuel and produces carbon dioxide. Smaller independent markets buy locally grown fruits and vegetables that spend more time ripening on the vine than traveling across the country—or the world. A growing movement encourages food labels to include information about how many miles the product traveled from the farm to the store. This would allow shoppers to purchase more locally grown produce and avoid food that's made a longer haul.

(not) enough!

According to the Organic Trade Association, the sale of organic foods increased 16 percent in 2005 alone, bringing in $13.8 million in sales. That's good, but not enough!

116 Grow native plants.

Go native! Using native plants when landscaping makes maintaining a healthy lawn even easier. Native plants are adapted to local climates and conditions so they don't need a lot of care to thrive. They have been flourishing for years without any help from humans. Native plants are accustomed to local pests so they do not depend on pesticides. Native plants are also acclimated to local weather conditions and rainfall meaning they don't need excessive watering or protection. And native plants will live longer than exotics, saving time and money, and conserving natural resources too.

▶ Local birds and butterflies are often attracted to native species, making a yard a haven to animals.

Rallying Cry!

"We have gained wetland acreage, thanks to the stewardship ethic of the nation's farmers and ranchers. Because of this achievement, USDA was able to help President Bush exceed his goal of improving, restoring, and protecting at least 3 million acres of wetlands in less than five years."

— MARK REY

Secretary of Natural Resources and Environment

117 Adopt an acre of wetlands.

Your support can help save these important wildlife areas. Check out *www.awf.org* to learn more about this type of ecosystem. Also, protect wetlands in your own region by monitoring city council meetings to see when the wetlands might be encroached upon by development. Attend meetings to voice your objections, and prepare ahead of time so you present a focused argument. Also, support local preservation organizations.

118 Organize an Earth Day cleanup.

Celebrate Earth Day. April 22nd is when the world's attention is focused on making our planet a healthier place for all to live. Organize a massive cleanup in conjunction with the holiday. Visit the day's official website—*www.earthday.net*—so you can coordinate your efforts with others across the globe. Other ways to help:

1. Sponsor an acre of rain forest. Make a forty-dollar donation in the name of someone for whom you would otherwise purchase a present. See *www.rainforestconcern.org*.

2. Volunteer your skills to Care 2 Make a Difference, an organization that works with the Wildlife Conservation Society and the Nature Conservancy to do good for specific environmental causes. Visit *www.care2.com* for volunteer opportunities.

3. Protect endangered species of birds. The Whooping Crane, the Mexican Spotted Owl, the Ivory-Billed Woodpecker, and the Puerto Rican Parrot, along with hundreds of other birds are in danger of becoming extinct. Find out more at *www.audubon.org/bird/watchlist/index.html*.

don't forget the ocean!

Do your part to clean our shores. Join the worldwide effort to clean up trash lying along the shorelines of the world's oceans, rivers, and lakes. For information, see *www.oceanconservancy.org*. Play a part in protecting ocean reefs. Pledge money to save a specific area of these underwater wonders and receive a deed to the reef section you are personally protecting. Visit *www.savenature.org* to purchase your patch.

THE PRESIDENT SAYS

"But Earth Day is not just an urgent call to action; it is a reminder that what is now a global effort began as a grassroots movement for change."

— BARACK OBAMA

119 Support alternative energy sources.

Many groups in the United States are looking to renewable energy sources—wind, water, and solar energy—for electricity. Find one whose mission matches your ideals and support it. Check out *www .supportalternativeenergy.com* for more. You can also determine your own impact on the environment by calculating the amount of carbon dioxide you produce. Websites such as *www.conservationfund.org* will do the calculations for you. Calculations are based on the size of your household, number of miles driven in what types of car, air miles flown, and the amount of garbage generated.

enough!
To date, twenty-three states and the District of Columbia have set standards for how much of their electricity must be generated by renewable sources.

THE PRESIDENT SAYS

"I believe that the U.S. can and should be a global leader in the development of alternative energy sources, such as ethanol and other biofuels, as well as wind and solar."

—BARACK OBAMA

120 Document illegal dumping.

Abandoned piles of household garbage, discarded appliances, old barrels, used tires, and demolition debris can threaten the health of humans, wildlife, and the environment. So don't turn a blind eye when you see it—call your local department of public works to report transgressions. Illegal dumping is a major problem that raises significant concerns about safety, property values, and quality of life in our communities. It also places a major economic burden on local government, which is typically responsible for cleaning up dump sites. Open dumps can pose the following health, safety, and environmental threats:

1. Fire and explosion
2. Injury to children playing in or around the dump site
3. Disease carried by mosquitoes, flies, and rodents
4. Contamination of bodies of water, groundwater, wells, and soil
5. Damage to plant and wildlife habitats
6. Decrease in the quality of life to nearby communities and residents

Do you need *more* reasons!?

THE PRESIDENT SAYS

"No one has the right to use America's rivers and America's waterways that belong to all the people, as a sewer. The banks of a river may belong to one man or one industry or one state, but the waters which flow between the banks should belong to all the people."

— LYNDON B. JOHNSON

121

Alert the media to local environmental issues.

If you notice a local environmental problem, address it yourself. If you run into bureaucratic red tape, contact local media outlets. Many newspapers, radio stations, and television stations list their personnel directories online, making it easier to find a specific person to contact. Likewise, if the media has covered a story, but you don't believe it was done fairly, contact the editor or a manager. List the items you took issue with and provide correct facts. Remember that if you want to maintain an ongoing relationship with the media, bullying them won't help.

122

Report environmental hazards to the EPA.

The Environmental Protection Agency (EPA) evaluates companies on their environmental performance using the National Environmental Performance Track, a program established in 2000 to recognize public and private institutions that go above and beyond the minimum environmental requirements. If you suspect a company is not following government guidelines, drop a dime! Log onto *www.epa.gov/epahome/postal.htm* and find the telephone numbers for your regional EPA office.

THE PRESIDENT SAYS

"A nation, like a person, has a mind—a mind that must be kept informed and alert, that must know itself, that understands the hopes and needs of its neighbors—all the other nations that live within the narrowing circle of the world."

— FRANKLIN D. ROOSEVELT

"He who passively accepts evil is as much involved in it as he who helps to perpetrate it. He who accepts evil without protesting against it is really cooperating with it."

— MARTIN LUTHER KING JR.

123 Protest developers threatening green spaces.

Although debated by many, urban sprawl is often blamed for destroying wildlife habitats, adding roads and cars, and usually requiring an expansion of infrastructure systems such as water, wastewater, and electricity. Development projects must go through rigorous approval processes, including environmental impact studies. Call your city council's office and ask to be put on their mailing lists for upcoming meetings. You can usually access an agenda prior to the meeting to see when the project will be evaluated and approved. Listen to the arguments presented and if appropriate, offer your comments and suggestions.

124

Spearhead a boycott of a business known for polluting the environment.

125

Write letters to your elected officials.

Some environmental issues are decided by individual states, not by the federal government. In that case, state lawmakers have more influence. If you aren't sure who your representatives or senators are, look up your state government's website. Your senators and representatives may have a local office in their district and/or an office in the state's capital, so try for a face-to-face meeting. Depending on the person's schedule in the legislature, you may receive a call back from an aide rather than the lawmaker you originally contacted. Don't take offense—they have administrative help to more quickly respond to constituents. Visit *www.speakout.com* for a wealth of information on all aspects of the legislative process and the best ways to communicate with legislators. The site also contains additional information on political activism.

Rallying Cry!

"It is time to make our representatives more responsive to the people who elect them."

— ARNOLD SCHWARZENEGGER

126

Identify any local environmental hazard— and fight it.

Take it upon yourself to right a wrong. Make calls, request change, and follow through.

enough!

The U.S. Conference of Mayors is just one coalition working to improve cities in a variety of ways. More than two hundred cities have pledged accordance with the Climate Protection Agreement, a pact that encourages each city to reduce greenhouse gas emissions by 7 percent from 1990 levels by the year 2012.

127 Live in an environmentally conscious city.

The EPA maintains an Air Quality Index (*www.airnow.gov*) that scores ozone and particulate matter for different cities across the United States. If you are looking for an official list, review the Green Guide Top 10 Green Cities, which is put out annually by the Green Guide Institute, an independent research organization that provides information for consumers so they can make informed environmental choices. Check out their website and the list at *www.the greenguide.com*.

Look for cities that encourage environmentally friendly transportation. Conscientious cities also:

★ Provide carpool lanes, dedicated bicycle lanes, walking trails, and sidewalks
★ Are designed to run efficiently without the need for individually owned vehicles
★ Already use or are making headway with alternative fuels such as biomass, geothermal, hydroelectric, solar, and wind

Search websites for information on cities that use alternative fuels, such as *www .sustainlane.us* and *www.eere.energy.gov*.

THE PRESIDENT SAYS

"The American people have a right to air that they and their children can breathe without fear."

— LYNDON B. JOHNSON

128 Live in an Energy Star state.

The EPA and the Department of Energy's Energy Star program created criteria to give homeowners and contractors guidelines and direction when looking for more sustainable approaches to construction. Energy Star rates homes, businesses, and household products for energy efficiency. In fifteen states, more than 20 percent of homes have qualified for the Energy Star label. The Energy Star website, *www .energystar.gov*, has more information.

savings star

In 2007, Energy Star helped Americans avoid energy that causes greenhouse gas emissions equal to 27 million cars, saving those citizens $16 billion on their utility bills.

Source: *www.energystar.gov*

129 Vote for green-minded candidates.

One of the most important political moves you can make is to vote. Politicians are elected as representatives, and they generally work to promote the beliefs of their constituents—the people they represent and the people who elected them. To get the most from your vote, know the issues and where the candidates stand. If you want to bring attention to a local issue or if you need a question answered, contact your local political leaders and regulators. Contact information should be in the phone book or available on the municipality's or agency's website.

 THE PRESIDENT SAYS

"Always vote for principle, though you may vote alone, and you may cherish the sweetest reflection that your vote is never lost."

—JOHN QUINCY ADAMS

130 Run for office yourself on a green platform.

Protecting the environment can be a very political issue. The foundation of the Green Party of the United States is based primarily on environmentalism and social justice. Similarly, the Greens/Green Party USA also promotes sustainability and a balance between people and nature. While these two parties focus primarily on the environment and other social issues, these issues are increasingly becoming a part of the platforms of more mainstream political parties. Consider joining a political organization in your area or volunteering for a candidate who makes the environment an important aspect of his or her campaign. You may be able to meet like-minded people in your area online at websites of political and activist organizations.

Get involved, gain knowledge, be proactive, and when you're ready, run for a local office in the Green Party—maybe you'll skyrocket to a presidential candidacy in no time!

"The use of solar energy has not been opened up because the oil industry does not own the sun."

—RALPH NADER

THE PRESIDENT SAYS

"When we got into office, the thing that surprised me the most was that things were as bad as we'd been saying they were."

—JOHN F. KENNEDY

KEEP
AMERICA
SMART

131.
Go to college.

99

132.
Get a master's degree.

100

133.
Learn a new technology.

100

134.
Master your worst subject.

101

135.
Read the classics.

101

136.
Turn off the TV two days a week.

102

137.
Take up the violin.

102

138.
Learn a new word each day.

103

139.
Solve a puzzle a day.

103

140.
Write a nonfiction book.

104

141.
Join your local library.

104

142.
Subscribe to news magazines.

105

143.
Exercise your brain.

105

144.
Join a book club.

106

145.

Host a book signing for your favorite author.

106

146.

Break a sweat.

107

147.

Use your imagination.

107

CHAPTER 11

EDUCATE A CHILD

109

148.

Start saving for your kid's education.

109

149.

Help a high school dropout get a GED.

110

150.

Write a letter of reference for a college student.

110

151.

Buy a child a book.

111

152.

Tutor youth in your hometown.

111

153.

Teach a child to read.

112

154.

Buy a computer for a local student.

112

155.

Volunteer for Junior Achievement.

113

156.

Participate in Bring a Child to Work Day.

113

157.

Help a disadvantaged kid in college.

114

158.

Support AmeriCorps.

114

CHAPTER 12
EDUCATE YOUR FELLOW AMERICANS
115

159.
Help a late adopter learn to use a computer.

115

160.
Teach at your local community college.

116

161.
Teach a class at a retirement village.

116

162.
Donate books to an assisted living facility.

117

163.
Teach an adult to read.

117

164.
Become a teacher.

118

165.
Endow a scholarship at your alma mater.

119

166.
Chaperone a field trip.

119

167.
Donate your newspaper to a local school.

120

168.
Join the PTA.

121

169.
Write a letter praising a good teacher.

122

170.
Celebrate Teacher Appreciation Week.

122

171.
Serve on your local school board.

123

172.
Support bonds for new schools.

124

EDUCATE YOURSELF

131 Go to college.

To become effective citizens with vision and determination, you need an education. If you're still in high school, work hard so you can win scholarships, or do whatever you have to do (community college, work-study programs, etc.) to get a higher education. If you're older and don't have a college education, it's never too late! Educate yourself and elevate our nation!

Here's another idea: Help an at-risk teen go to college. Work with other professionals in your community to assist at-risk youth who may have the intelligence to do well in college but not understand the process or know how to find the resources to make it happen. You can make a difference in their lives.

college degree = money

Americans with bachelor's degrees earn about one-third more than their peers who do not finish college and nearly twice as much as those with only a high school diploma.

Source: Department of Education

 **THE PRESIDENT SAYS**

"Leadership and learning are indispensable to each other."

— JOHN F. KENNEDY

As written in the speech he was due to deliver in Dallas the day he was assassinated, November 22, 1963

132 Get a master's degree.

As India and China and many other emerging nations gain on us, it's more important than ever that we remember how far higher education has brought us as a nation. Joe the Plumber may be a perfectly good small businessman—and they're important—but we need Joe the Green Technology Scientist, and Joe the Cancer Researcher, and Joe the Technology Inventor, and Joe the Media Specialist, and—well, you get the idea. Education is a good thing!

> *"What a computer is to me is the most remarkable tool that we have ever come up with. It's the equivalent of a bicycle for our minds."*
>
> —STEVE JOBS
> Cofounder of Apple

133 Learn a new technology.

Like it or not, we are all moving into the twenty-first century, and America needs to regain its status as the most innovative nation on the planet. Do your part and stay on top of technology; in fact, embrace new technology—buy an iPhone, log onto Twitter, create a website, release a podcast, Skype your daughter at college, get a mini-laptop, go completely digital, get hip.

134 Master your worst subject.

Education is never a bad thing, and studies have shown that the more education you receive, the better your mental acuity—and the longer you will retain it. Take a class that challenges your thought processes, rather than something with which you're already familiar. Most community colleges and universities offer continuing education classes on a wide variety of subjects, and many sessions are held at night to accommodate people who work during the day. And, remember, choose a challenging subject, something that forces you to think or flexes brain cells you haven't used for eons.

135 Read the classics.

Read as much as you can and focus on works that challenge you. The latest potboiler may be a fun read, but it's probably as mentally challenging as a *Dick and Jane* primer. You can give your brain a workout by reading a literary classic you've always meant to tackle or by reading a nonfiction book on a topic you're interested in but know nothing about. Read carefully, with memory and recall in mind. To help assimilate this new information, discuss it with friends.

Rallying Cry!

"'Which books should I read first?' The answer to that is 'The great patterning works of world literature and culture, the poems and stories that have shaped civilization.' Without a knowledge of the Greek myths, the Bible, ancient history, the world's folktales and fairy tales, one can never fully understand half the literature of later ages. Homer tells us about Ulysses in *The Odyssey*; then Dante, Tennyson, James Joyce, Wallace Stevens, and Eudora Welty add to, enrich, and subvert that story in great works of their own. The classics are important because they are always being renewed."

— MICHAEL DIRDA

Pulitzer Prize–winning critic and author of *Bound to Please: An Extraordinary One-Volume Literary Education: Essays on Great Writers and Their Books*

136 Turn off the TV two days a week.

Medical studies have proven that the one activity that led to less brain stimulation and increased risk of Alzheimer's was watching television. Listening to music, socializing, talking on the phone, visiting friends, and attending church services lowered the risk of Alzheimers, while reading books, studying a foreign language, and traveling were even more beneficial. It's a matter of engaging in life fully, having goals, having fun, and being interested in your surroundings, in other people, and in yourself. Sitting in front of the television is not the best way to enjoy your life—or to become an active citizen.

"If it weren't for electricity we'd all be watching television by candlelight."

— GEORGE GOBEL

137 Take up the violin.

Brain specialists have long known that learning to play a musical instrument teaches the brain new patterns and stimulates wide areas of the cerebral cortex. In other words, learning a musical instrument, at any age, can be helpful in developing and activating temporal lobe neurons, which primes the mental pump.

THE PRESIDENT SAYS

"Well, I don't have much job security."

— BILL CLINTON

In 1992, on why he still plays the saxophone

138 Learn a new word each day.

Flexing your brain cells with a few basic word-play exercises warms up your mental engine. Words are fun; they expand your mind. Pick up your dictionary and pick out five words you don't know. Commit their definition to memory, and then see if you can recite their definitions from memory the next day. And then learn five more. As you persevere, you'll soon discover that the task of committing words to memory will become increasingly easier to achieve and more satisfying.

139 Solve a puzzle a day.

Stimulate your brain by doing puzzles, such as the daily crossword puzzle, anagrams, find-a-word, and maze games. Puzzles are a great way to strengthen and maintain several different areas of cognitive function, including memory and visual-spatial areas. You can buy inexpensive puzzle books and they're a great way to kill time while waiting in line or for an appointment. Crosswords, word-search puzzles, sudoku, and other puzzles are all good ways to occupy your mind without stressing it. These activities will keep your brain fit, too.

140 Write a nonfiction book.

Write your autobiography! This can be a rewarding activity in that you preserve your life experiences for the benefit of other family members and exercise your brain in the process. Recalling previous events requires a strong memory (which may be aided by going through photo albums, letters, etc.), and the act of writing improves visual-spatial skills. Also, consider writing about something that stirs your soul or fires up your passions. Use all that knowledge you've accumulated and put it to good use educating others. Or, research a completely foreign subject and educate yourself, as you write a book about it.

"When I was a kid and the other kids were home watching Leave It to Beaver, my father and stepmother were marching me off to the library."

— OPRAH WINFREY

141 Join your local library.

Still the best value in the country! Local libraries are treasure troves of information and free entertainment. They are also meeting places, and a nice place to spend an afternoon reading. Visit yours often—and better yet, volunteer at your local library. And think of ideas for mini-seminars on your special field and how you could interest children in learning more about what you do, or what they might like to do in the future.

142 Subscribe to news magazines.

Instead of reading junk, read books and magazines and newspapers that offer in-depth, factual, balanced reporting on the critical issues of our day which will enlighten you as a human being and a citizen. We need to be following what is happening around the world and how Americans fit into the picture. We all have a responsibility to educate ourselves on an ongoing basis—it makes us strong.

THE PRESIDENT SAYS

"What's a man got to do to get in the top fifty?"

— BILL CLINTON

Reacting to a survey of journalists that ranked the Monica Lewinsky scandal as the 53rd most significant story of the century

143 Exercise your brain.

According to Dr. Frank Lawlis in *The IQ Answer*, an idle brain loses brainpower. Just as physical exercise generates strength in various parts of the body, mental exercise builds strength in various parts of the brain. Lawlis recommends bridge, chess, poker, bingo, charades, and games favored by Mensa, an organization of brainiacs (those who rank in the top 2 percent when it comes to IQ), such as Brainstrain, Cityscape, Cube Checkers, Doubles Wild, Finish Lines, and many more that can be found in American Mensa Library. America needs your brain to be as sharp as a tack and ready to take on new challenges. Come on, play already!

CALL TO Online Action!

Smart People
According to Mensa, some 100,000 smart people in 100 countries across the globe are Mensans. If you think you can make that top 2 percent IQ cut, check out *www.mensa .org* and see for yourself.

144 Join a book club.

This has the triple bonus. Most book clubs pick challenging books and set a deadline for reading them. Part of the fun is analyzing a book's theme, characterizations, plot, and other concepts that may not be familiar to you, but that will be a lot of fun, as well as mentally challenging. Also, groups typically gather for discussions, offering you opportunities to socialize, engage in conversation, and invigorate yourself. It's also likely to help you stay contemporary, and keep up with what's going on in the world. Join a book club; it's a win-win-win situation.

top ten book club favorites

1. *Peace Like a River* by Leif Enger
2. *The Shack* by William P. Young
3. *The Spirit Catches You and You Fall Down* by Anne Fadiman
4. *The Next Thing on My List: A Novel* by Jill Smolinski
5. *The Thirteenth Tale* by Diane Setterfield
6. *Water for Elephants: A Novel* by Sara Gruen
7. *A Thread of Grace* by Mary Doria Russell
8. *Three Cups of Tea: One Man's Mission to Promote Peace . . . One School at a Time* by Greg Mortenson and David Oliver Relin
9. *One Thousand White Women: The Journals of May Dodd: A Novel* by Jim Fergus
10. *The Glass Castle* by Jeannette Walls

Source: *www.bookmovement.com*, as of November 2008

145 Host a book signing for your favorite author.

After eight years when the arts—and everything they offer to our country—were ignored, if not outright insulted and denigrated, do your part to light up the neighborhood by inviting all your friends and family to attend a book signing for your favorite (probably starving) author. Make it a celebratory occasion and one that encourages others to love books as much as you do. We have a wealth of talented writers in this great nation: Adopt one and make their day.

146 Break a sweat.

Physical exercise helps us lose excess weight, increase our physical strength, and reduce stress. Physical exercise increases the blood flow to the brain, bringing oxygen and nutrients and taking away waste products. Aerobic exercise helps get the blood coursing through your system, carrying oxygen and glucose to your brain—two substances the brain needs in order to function.

► The U.S. federal guidelines for exercise say that getting at least thirty minutes a day most days a week will help prevent heart disease, osteoporosis, diabetes, obesity, and now, perhaps, Alzheimer's.

147 Use your imagination.

Creativity is what happens in your brain when you relax and allow your brain to birth new thoughts, new ways of seeing, or new ways of doing. According to Dr. Frank Lawlis, author of *The IQ Answer*, when you enter a creative state, your brain enters the theta state in which your frontal lobe shuts down, allowing other areas to light up. In this creative state, the occipital lobe (imagery) and the temporal lobe (memory) activate. In effect, your brain goes into a sort of blissful, hypnotic state that often results in creative works of art. Achieving a creative state of mind can be almost as restorative as deep sleep. So challenge your brain by releasing it to work its magic.

cheer up
According to author David Rakel, in his 2002 book, *Integrative Medicine*, more than 10,000 trials have examined the relationship between exercise and mood, showing that exercise may be just as effective in treating depression as psychotherapy.

"Imagination is more important than knowledge."

—ALBERT EINSTEIN

EDUCATE A CHILD

148 Start saving for your kid's education.

Because credit markets have tightened up, far more parents will be financing their children's education. Even if you are strapped for money, investing a small sum each month can add up. It might not pay for college, but accumulated savings can significantly reduce the costs, and thereby the amount of money you or your child will need to borrow. Consider the following table, which shows how quickly savings can accumulate.

enough!
According to the College Board's *Trends in College Pricing*, the 2008–2009 average total costs increased 6.4 percent for public four-year colleges, 5.9 percent for private four-year colleges, and 4.7 percent for two-year colleges.

HOW SAVINGS ACCUMULATE, ON AVERAGE				
Length of time	*$15 per week*	*$25 per week*	*$35 per week*	*$50 per week*
Two years	1,676	2,793	3,910	5,585
Five years	4,673	7,788	10,903	15,576
Ten years	11,303	18,839	26,374	37,678
Fifteen years	20,712	34,520	48,329	69,041

149 Help a high school dropout get a GED.

The GED tests measure high school–level skills and knowledge. The GED credential offers adults who dropped out of high school a second chance at attending college or pursuing a career. Work with your local school district to locate high school dropouts and write to them, offering your assistance in helping them acquire a GED. You could also post announcements offering your help at your local library. Each state may have its own test and requirements. For the most accurate information on GEDs, log on to the American Council on Education website at *www.acenet.edu.*

"We have come to identify quality in a college not by whom it serves but by how many students it excludes. Instead, let us be the fulfillers of dreams."

—ROBERT J. KIBBEE
City University of New York

150 Write a letter of reference for a college student.

Work with other professionals in your community to assist students who may not understand the college application process or how to find resources to acquire impressive letters of reference. Once you have a list of professionals willing to help, contact your local high schools and offer to help those aspiring to study in your field, and try to match up others with professionals who could add weight to their application. You can make a real difference in their lives.

151 Buy a child a book.

Every child loves a book, but sadly, we have too many children in our country who don't have books in their homes—if they have a home. Stock up on your favorites, or your children's favorites, and donate them to local homeless shelters, women's shelters, daycare centers, and anyplace that provides free clothing or necessities to children.

152 Tutor youth in your hometown.

Put your education and your accumulated knowledge to good use—be a mentor to one or more students. They can benefit greatly from your guidance. This may be especially true of children living in single-parent households.

Other ideas:

★ Help out children who live on the streets. You can offer them choices, skills, and opportunities for a better life and healthier future. Check out *www.streetkids.org*.

★ Volunteer with National Children's Coalition, which helps at-risk kids who are runaways, abused, or addicted. Help where others have given up. For more information, see *www.child.net*.

Rallying Cry!

"There are many little ways to enlarge your child's world. Love of books is the best of all."

— JACQUELINE KENNEDY ONASSIS

▶ **Whether they are attending primary school, middle school, or high school, students could benefit greatly from having an older, responsible person guiding them and helping them master difficult subjects.**

153 Teach a child to read.

Many local libraries offer programs that match children in need of tutors with volunteers. Teaching a child to read is not only a great deal of fun, it gives a real leg up to those who may lag behind if they don't receive one-on-one individual attention. There's nothing more glorious than seeing a child light up with pride when he or she has learned something—particularly something that opens up a whole new world. As your student progresses, reward him or her with a book to match his or her new skills.

> *"There is more treasure in books than in all the pirate's loot on Treasure Island."*
>
> —WALT DISNEY

154 Buy a computer for a local student.

Imagine the thrill you'll give to a lucky scholarship student whose parents don't have the funds for a computer. If you can't afford a new computer, look for used ones, or donate your used computer or laptop when you upgrade. Also, if you know a lot about computers, you could help set up a school's computer lab. Contact a local school and put your technological know-how to use. Most schools do not have an in-house IT professional, so by volunteering you're helping children's education and saving the school system money.

geeks need only apply

Kids on their way to college need more high-tech skills than ever. They need to be what's now known as "new media literate," as well as old-media (read: books) literate. They must master research and technical skills as well as written skills—and be able to understand, communicate, and manipulate visual, audio, and textual information.
Source: MacArthur Foundation

155 Volunteer for Junior Achievement.

Encouraging children to use their creativity, set goals, reach for their dreams, and master achievement can only benefit us as a nation. By sharing your expertise and offering them instruction, motivation, and recognition, you will be offering priceless opportunities for them to learn how to be productive contributors to our society. Some may even become world leaders. Though cliché, the old adage that our children are our future is true. Let's not short-change them. Find out how to get involved on *www.ja.org*.

enough!

In its seventh annual "Teens and Entrepreneurship" poll, Junior Achievement has found that thirteen- to eighteen-year-olds are less interested in starting their own businesses than they were a year ago. In 2007, 67 percent of teens indicated an interest in entrepreneurship; in 2008 that number declined to 60 percent—perhaps as a result of the stagnating economy.

156 Participate in Bring a Child to Work Day.

If you don't have a child at home anymore, call your local school or church and offer to adopt one for the day. Or, ask friends and family if they know of any children that would like to learn more about your profession and offer them a unique view into your daily life at work. Another idea: Offer to participate in career day at your local high school. Volunteer to talk about your career and inspire young teens to enter your field of work.

"The equal or other half of this is 'Take Our Sons Home Day,' since they have been equally deprived of exposure to what work the home requires."

—GLORIA STEINEM

Founding president, *Ms.* Foundation for Women and co-creator of Take Our Daughters to Work Day

Donate to a Kid in Need
Make a donation to the National Center for Children in Poverty to help these kids receive the financial support they need. Visit the center's website at *www.nccp.org.*

157

Help a disadvantaged kid in college.

Offer to help with expenses or offer an empty room in your house to a college student who must live off campus. Although that young person will be busy with studies and perhaps gone a lot to attend classes, he or she may enrich your life in ways you cannot imagine, especially if from a different country and culture.

read this and weep

Only 8.6 percent of America's disadvantaged youth earn bachelor's degrees by age twenty-four, compared to 7.1 percent in 1975. Which means that the 32 percent disparity between low-income kids who go to college and wealthy kids who go to college has remained virtually unchanged in more than thirty years.
Source: Postsecondary Education Opportunity

158 Support AmeriCorps.

Each year, AmeriCorps (*www.americorps .org*) offers 75,000 opportunities for adults of all ages and backgrounds to serve through a network of partnerships with local and national nonprofit groups. Adults commit to spending a year living in disadvantaged communities across America, addressing critical needs, such as helping to:

★ Tutor and mentor disadvantaged youth
★ Improve health services
★ Build affordable housing
★ Teach computer skills
★ Clean parks and streams
★ Manage or operate afterschool programs
★ Help communities respond to disasters
★ Build organizational capacity

159 Help a late adopter learn to use a computer.

Technology has grown so fast that many people haven't been able to adjust as fast as the rest of us—and it's not all senior citizens. Contact a few retirement homes and women's shelters and offer your free technology knowledge. Showing someone how to operate a few simple programs will help your students immensely, whether they want to:

★ Stay in touch with loved ones
★ Get a job
★ Try doing a crossword online

You'll have a waiting list in no time!

> *"Crooks are early adopters."*
>
> — CRAIG NEWMARK
> Founder of craigslist.org

▶ In his groundbreaking 2001 essay, "The Law of Accelerating Returns," Ray Kurzweil explains that "an analysis of the history of technology shows that technological change is exponential, contrary to the common-sense 'intuitive linear' view. So we won't experience 100 years of progress in the twenty-first century—it will be more like 20,000 years of progress (at today's rate)."

160
Teach at your local community college.

We all have special knowledge we could share. Plus, it's a great way to give back to your community and to keep you active. Also, there's an old adage known to teachers that it takes three years of teaching to truly master a subject. If you have something you'd like to learn, or a subject you'd like to learn more about, you will never learn a topic better than when you start teaching it.

"Good teaching is one-fourth preparation and three-fourths theater."

— GAIL GODWIN

161
Teach a class at a retirement village.

Volunteer at a senior citizen center. Visit a senior citizen housing complex and offer to teach a workshop on a subject you know well. Such complexes often have a library or a music room or a place where seniors can gather for such a presentation. You will be sharing your knowledge with people who maybe can't get out to lectures like they used to, and you may well have a captive audience of people intensely interested in your subject.

THE PRESIDENT SAYS

"Modern cynics and skeptics . . . see no harm in paying those to whom they entrust the minds of their children a smaller wage than is paid to those to whom they entrust the care of their plumbing."

— JOHN F. KENNEDY

162 Donate books to an assisted living facility.

You can also donate books and magazines to homeless shelters, women's shelters, churches, doctor's offices, and even local libraries, if you have unique, specialized magazines that they might not have.

CALL TO
Online Action!

Support Seniors
Support nonprofit orga-
nizations that aid senior
citizens, such as the
American Association
of Homes and Services
for the Aging. Visit *www.
aahsa.org* for more
information.

163 Teach an adult to read.

Many immigrants want desperately to learn to read in their new language. Post notices (in whatever language you may know, or in English) offering free tutoring on local grocery store bulletin boards or places they may frequent. You can also contact local community centers and libraries, as they often offer language courses where you'll find people (immigrants and nonim-migrants) eager to learn how to read or to vastly improve their reading skills.

read this and weep

- 42 million American adults are illiterate; 50 million read at a fourth-grade level.
- The ranks of functionally illiterate adult Americans rise some 2.25 million every year.
- One in five graduating high school seniors are functionally illiterate.

Source: National Right to Read Foundation

164 Become a teacher.

Teaching is a special calling. Here are seven reasons why teaching can be a great profession:

1. You can help children achieve their full potential.
2. Children are our nation's future!
3. Our country desperately needs good teachers.
4. It's a ball. As Art Linkletter proved long ago, students say the darndest things.
5. You help shape positive attitudes and values. You often spend more time with children than their parents do.
6. It keeps you young. You'll also be hip.
7. You run the show. Not many jobs provide an individual with so much room to be creative and autonomous each day.
8. It gives you more time to be with your children.
9. Job security. These days, teachers are a scarce commodity, and you can move around easier once you're established as an effective teacher.
10. Summers off, and long winter and spring vacations.

"I am learning all the time. The tombstone will be my diploma."

— EARTHA KITT

THE PRESIDENT SAYS

"A third place to build the Great Society is in the classrooms of America. There your children's lives will be shaped. Our society will not be great until every young mind is set free to scan the farthest reaches of thought and imagination."

— LYNDON B. JOHNSON

165

Endow a scholarship at your alma mater.

If you've done well in life, perhaps it had everything to do with where you attended high school or college. Give back by establishing a scholarship at your alma mater and help other aspiring students achieve their dreams. When you fund an endowment, it must be used to your specification—you can give it to a student from your hometown, an art history major, or one from a low-income family. It's a lovely way to be helpful and to become a permanent part of your former school's legacy.

166

Chaperone a field trip.

Whether it's your own child or perhaps a niece or nephew, take a day off work and visit one of the fascinating places kids go to learn outside the classroom. Remember how exciting those trips were as a kid? Relive some of that excitement while lending a classroom teacher a hand keeping track of all the youngsters. Come on, who doesn't want to tour a crayon factory? Don't forget your permission slip!

THE PRESIDENT SAYS

"We must do more to make sure education meets the needs of our children and the demands of the future. First and foremost, we must continue to hold students, teachers, and schools to the highest standards. We must ensure students can demonstrate competence to be promoted and to graduate. Teachers must also demonstrate competence, and we should be prepared to reward the best ones, and remove those who don't measure up, fairly and expeditiously."

— BILL CLINTON

167

Donate your newspaper to a local school.

Along with the shortage of books in homes these days is the lack of a daily newspaper. Many kids aren't familiar with the concept, since their parents probably read news online. If you still get a newspaper delivered, consider using a program that allows you to "donate" it to a school when you would have otherwise suspended delivery, like when on vacation. The newspaper company usually takes care of all the details; call yours for information.

The students can read about current events, learn about the stock market and meteorology, and get their fingers stained with ink—the old-fashioned way of reading news! It only costs you pennies and you won't come home to a stack of yellowed pages filled with old news.

"It's amazing that the amount of news that happens in the world every day always just exactly fits the newspaper."

— JERRY SEINFELD

168 Join the PTA.

The Parent Teacher Association is the largest volunteer child advocacy association in the nation, providing parents and families with a powerful voice to speak on behalf of every child and the best tools to help their children be safe, healthy, and successful—in school and in life. Log on to the national website *www.pta.org* for inspiration and then sign up to participate. If you've got political aspirations, you may want to chart a path onto the city council and mayorship—it worked for Sarah Palin.

"My mother was the president of the PTA at every school I attended."

—VERNON JORDAN JR.
African-American lawyer
and activist

Ways to participate:

1. *Join your local unit.* Use the look-up feature on the national website to find your local PTA, then contact the school or PTA president, and join. For more information, contact your state PTA.
2. *Join the national PTA.* If you are concerned with advocacy, or want more materials than a local PTA membership provides, consider joining the national PTA.
3. *Start a unit.* If there is no parent group activity at your school now, or your existing parent group wants to realize all the benefits of PTA membership, contact the national PTA, and they will help you get started.

169 Write a letter praising a good teacher.

We all know that teachers are underpaid and overworked. And these days, many of them pay for school supplies for their students! Take a few minutes out of your day to write a letter alerting the school board to what a particular teacher does that makes him or her special and respected. Once you begin, you may find it so rewarding that you'll find time once a month or so to write another letter, and to encourage your friends to write letters. The teachers will thank you for it!

> *"The good teacher makes the poor student good and the good student superior."*
>
> — MARVA COLLINS
>
> Famous educator who applied classical education successfully with impoverished students

170 Celebrate Teacher Appreciation Week.

The first full week in May is celebrated as Teacher Appreciation Week. That Tuesday is the official Teacher Appreciation Day. Honor your favorite teachers—present and past—by sending a thank-you card. For teachers still teaching, buy school supplies or art supplies for their students. They and their students will love you for it. Log on to the National Teacher Association's website at *www.nea.org/teacherday* for more information and to sign up for their nationwide "Thank-You Card Project," helping to create a "larger-than-life mural" of thanks.

171 Serve on your local school board.

The National School Board Association has a wealth of information on how school boards function. Log on to their website, *www.nsba.org,* to study up on the key issues they face. To find out how to become a school board member in your community, look under their "Resource" link to find state requirements. Consider these five reasons that the school board, which represents your community's beliefs and values, should be the decision maker in today's schools:

1. Your school board looks out for children—first and foremost. Education is not a line item in your school board's budget—it is the *only* item.
2. Your school board is the advocate for your community when decisions are made about your children's education.
3. Your school board sets the standard for achievement and works with the superintendent to establish a valid process for measuring student success and, when necessary, shifting resources to ensure goals are achieved.
4. Your school board is accessible to you and accountable for the performance of the schools in your district.
5. Your school board is your community's education watchdog, ensuring that taxpayers get the most for their tax dollars.

enough!
Public education is a $423 billion business. In the majority of districts, school boards have taxing authority. That direct oversight—and responsibility—should rest with someone whose first priority is a child's education.

THE
PRESIDENT
SAYS

"I don't think much of a man who is not wiser today than he was yesterday."

—ABRAHAM LINCOLN

172 Support bonds for new schools.

The National Clearinghouse for Educational Facilities provides information on bond programs that fund the construction of school buildings and information on conducting bond campaigns. Go to *www.edfacilities.org* to learn more. The basics you should know:

1. As a voter in a district, you vote on every bond separately from every other question on the ballot.
2. Bonds are for specific money uses, usually for capital needs, new equipment, new classroom and administration buildings, parking lots, football fields, swimming pools, etc., but they can be issued for other purposes, such as teachers' raises.
3. School bonds are like any other kinds of bonds: They are promissory notes. The legislature sets a limit, based on the assessed value of the taxable property (usually 10 percent).
4. If the majority of the voters in the district vote no, the schools can't issue the bonds.
5. Bonds earn interest, perhaps 6 to 6.5 percent. But that also means that the voters/property owners in the district have to pay that interest.
6. Bonds are paid off through property taxes.

Rallying Cry!

"Genius without education is like silver in the mine."

— BENJAMIN FRANKLIN

THE PRESIDENT SAYS

"Upon the subject of education, not presuming to dictate any plan or system respecting it, I can only say that I view it as the most important subject which we as a people may be engaged in. That everyone may receive at least a moderate education appears to be an objective of vital importance."

— ABRAHAM LINCOLN

PART
FOUR

KEEP
AMERICA
CULTURED

186.
Write a song.

138

187.
Write a play.

139

188.
Write a novel.

139

189.
Learn a new dance.

140

190.
Learn to play an instrument.

140

191.
Take a photography class.

141

192.
Learn to paint.

141

193.
Throw a pot.

141

194.
Perform at a poetry slam.

142

195.
Learn a lost art.

142

CHAPTER 15

SHARE YOUR PASSION

143

196.
Teach your art or craft to local schoolchildren.

143

197.
Mentor an aspiring artist or writer.

144

198.
Teach a child your favorite poem.

144

199.
Sing in a choir.

145

200.

Take a kid to a local children's museum.

145

201.

Start a children's playhouse.

146

202.

Send a kid to summer music camp.

146

203.

Join your local theater group.

147

204.

Join the local photographer's guild.

147

205.

Host a crafts event at a retirement home.

148

206.

Ask your grandmother to teach you to knit.

148

207.

Take a child to a Renaissance Fair.

149

208.

Play in a local band.

149

CHAPTER 16

SUPPORT THE ARTS

151

209.

Support the Cultural Bill of Rights.

151

210.

Host an exhibit for an artist at your workplace.

152

211.

Hire a poet for a creativity workshop at work.

152

212.

Become a member of your local museum.

153

213.

Turn an extra room into a studio for an artist.

153

214.

Swap your own professional services for original artwork.

154

215.

Host a fundraiser for your favorite arts organization.

154

216.

Donate a product or service as a prize for an auction.

155

217.

Organize an open studios event for an arts community.

155

218.

Organize a wall mural painting in your community.

156

219.

Fight to keep art and music education in your local schools.

156

220.

Support the National Endowment for the Arts.

157

IMMERSE YOURSELF IN THE ARTS

173 Watch PBS.

Masterpiece. Great Performances. Sesame Street. If you're looking for a shot of culture, you don't have to look any further than your local Public Broadcasting Station. From Shakespeare to Sherlock Holmes, Renée Fleming to Bob Dylan, Freud to Frida Kahlo, you'll find a wealth of programming guaranteed to enlighten and entertain you and your family.

And if you're thinking that it's all British mysteries and sitcoms, think again. What's more American than a Ken Burns documentary, Alan Alda hosting *Scientific American,* or *Live from Lincoln Center*?

enough!

Republicans have cut more than $115 million in funding for the Corporation for Public Broadcasting since 2006—and more cuts are up for discussion. The rationale: PBS's "un-American" liberal bias.

▶ More than 65 million people in 40 million households watch public television either on-air or online during an average week, while the majority of American households (55 percent)—nearly 109 million people—watch over-the-air public television in a month.

174 Visit your local museum.

Move over, Metropolitan Museum of Art. You don't have to wait until you're in the big city to visit a museum. There are thousands of museums in America. From the Mystic Seaport Museum in Mystic, Connecticut, to the Pacific Tsunami Museum in Hilo, Hawaii, you can find a museum wherever you are—and whatever your preferred aesthetic. Check out the Virtual Library's USA Museums Database for more at *http://icom.museum/vlmp/usa.html.*

there's a museum for everything

- The Liberace Museum, Las Vegas, NV
- Dr. Pepper Museum, Waco, TX
- National Cowboy Hall of Fame, Oklahoma City, OK
- Studebaker Museum, South Bend, IN
- The Hippie Museum, Summerton, AL
- World Kite Museum, Long Beach, WA
- Wild Turkey Center and Museum, Edgefield, SC
- Rosalie Whyel Museum of Doll Art, Bellevue, WA
- Red Baron Museum, Marshall, MN
- Robert A. Paselk Scientific Instrument Museum, Arcata, CA

175 Listen to NPR.

Car Talk. All Things Considered. Fresh Air with Terry Gross. An American Life. A Prairie Home Companion. Need we say more? Who is already listening? 26 million Americans every week and counting.

176 See an opera.

Porgy and Bess. West Side Story. Nixon in China. These classic American operas are singing proof that opera is alive and well in the United States. In fact, our nation now boasts 125 opera companies—more than Germany or Italy. According to Opera America, some 20 million Americans go to the opera every year—roughly as many as attend NFL football games. So go see what all the singing is about—and prepare to be blown away.

177 Hang out at a poetry slam.

This is not your mother's poetry reading. Forget *Song of Hiawatha*. Think *Howl* meets hip hop. By most accounts, this all-American art form started in 1984 when Marc Smith hosted the first poetry slam at Chicago's Get Me High Lounge. Now the poetry slam has spread all over the world—and it has its own national competition, the National Poetry Slam, in which some eighty teams from across the nation compete. So check out your local poetry slam—and get slammed.

top ten operas

These are the ten most performed operas in North America:

1. *Madama Butterfly* by Giacomo Puccini
2. *La Bohème* by Giacomo Puccini
3. *La Traviata* by Giuseppe Verdi
4. *Carmen* by Georges Bizet
5. *The Barber of Seville* by Gioacchino Rossini
6. *The Marriage of Figaro* by Wolfgang Amadeus Mozart
7. *Don Giovanni* by Wolfgang Amadeus Mozart
8. *Tosca* by Giacomo Puccini
9. *Rigoletto* by Giuseppe Verdi
10. *The Magic Flute* by Wolfgang Amadeus Mozart

178 Go to a concert.

Nowhere in the world are there more opportunities than in America to hear live music. From jazz and classical to country and rock and everything in between, there's music for everyone. Enjoy!

179

Attend the ballet.

180 Take an arts vacation.

This year, go on a vacation you'll always remember—and can take home with you:

★ Photograph wildlife in Alaska.
★ Master the art of Cajun and Creole cooking in New Orleans.
★ Write your memoir on Cape Cod.
★ Learn to sculpt at the historic Rising Wolf Ranch in Montana.
★ Paint a landscape in the *plein air* tradition on beautiful Block Island in Rhode Island.

CALL TO
Online Action!

Check out *www.infohub.com* for more arts vacations. You can search by region or type of vacation you'd like to take.

181

Go to your local book and storytelling festivals.

If you love books, you'll love book and storytelling events. Old stories, children's stories, stories written by cowboys and griots and spoken aloud by storytellers . . . you'll find it all at one of these festivals.

TEN BOOK FESTIVALS YOU'LL LOVE

- ★ Miami Book Fair
- ★ Harlem Book Fair
- ★ Boston International Antiquarian Book Fair
- ★ LitQuake: San Francisco's Literary Festival
- ★ Los Angeles Latino Book and Family Festival
- ★ *Los Angeles Times* Festival of Books
- ★ Louisiana Book Festival
- ★ Maine Festival of the Book
- ★ Montana Festival of the Book
- ★ Wisconsin Book Festival

TEN STORYTELLING FESTIVALS YOU'LL LOVE

- ★ Bay Area Storytelling Festival
- ★ Bellingham Storytelling Festival
- ★ Extreme Trail Tales: An Iditarod Event
- ★ Hoosier Storytelling Festival
- ★ Talk Story Festival
- ★ Mariposa Storytelling Festival
- ★ Missouri River Storytelling Festival
- ★ Montana Storytelling Roundup
- ★ National Black Storytelling Festival and Conference
- ★ National Storytelling Festival

"The love of learning, the sequestered nooks, And all the sweet serenity of books."

— HENRY WADSWORTH LONGFELLOW

THE PRESIDENT SAYS

"Let us welcome controversial books and controversial authors."

— JOHN F. KENNEDY

> *"Stand-up comedy is transient. History shows that you can stand up for so long; after that, you're asked to sit down."*
>
> —STEVE MARTIN

182 Check out a local comedy club.

If the world were a comedy club, then we Americans would be the kings of comedy. We do humor right in this country. And every community has its clowns, so check out your local funny guys—and keep on laughing.

183 See an independent film.

The independent film is alive and well in America. But for movies like *Juno* and *Sideways* to continue to get made, we need to support the theaters that run indie films. Don't wait for the DVD . . . see an indie tonight!

TOP-GROSSING INDEPENDENT FILMS

1. *Star Wars*
2. *The Passion of the Christ*
3. *Blair Witch Project*
4. *Juno*
5. *No Country for Old Men*
6. *My Big Fat Greek Wedding*
7. *Pulp Fiction*
8. *Crouching Tiger, Hidden Dragon*
9. *Hot Fuzz*
10. *Little Miss Sunshine*
11. *Brokeback Mountain*
12. *Sideways*

THE PRESIDENT SAYS

> "We must never forget that art is not a form of propaganda; it is a form of truth."
>
> —JOHN F. KENNEDY

BECOME AN ARTIST YOURSELF

184 Write your autobiography.

Everyone has a unique American story to tell. Maybe it's time you told yours. Check out these wonderful autobiographical novels by your fellow Americans for inspiration:

★ *The Human Comedy* by William Saroyan
★ *The Heart of a Woman* by Maya Angelou
★ *The Bell Jar* by Sylvia Plath
★ *Farewell to Manzanar* by Jeanne Wakatsuki Houston and James D. Houston
★ *A Summer Life* by Gary Soto
★ *A Boy's Life* by Tobias Wolff
★ *The Things They Carried* by Tim O'Brien
★ *The Autobiography of Benjamin Franklin* by Benjamin Franklin
★ *Dreams from My Father* by Barack Obama

"I'm writing an unauthorized autobiography."

—STEVEN WRIGHT

185 Create a new recipe.

America is the melting pot of cuisines as well as peoples. Time to add your own spices and flavors to the mix. Slip on an apron and:

★ Modernize one of your grandmother's recipes.
★ Create a hybrid dish combining your various cultural traditions.
★ Make a new holiday dessert.
★ Try a new variation of an old classic.
★ Take one of your favorite ethnic dishes and make it your own.

"Noncooks think it's silly to invest two hours' work in two minutes' enjoyment; but if cooking is evanescent, so is the ballet."

— JULIA CHILD

186 Write a song.

Songs are shortcuts to the human heart. If you think you aren't musical enough to write your own, think again. You don't have to read music or even play an instrument to write a song. Irving Berlin, known as "America's Songwriter," wrote such classics as "God Bless America," "White Christmas," and "There's No Business Like Show Business," yet he apparently never learned to read music beyond a very basic level! Start small—write only lyrics or only a tune.

"Country music is three chords and the truth."

— HARLAN HOWARD
The Dean of Nashville Songwriters

187 Write a play.

If you love the theater, try your hand at writing a stage play. Community playhouses are always looking for new works to produce; check out *www.aact.org* for a list of theaters and submission guidelines. You can also arrange to have your work read by professional actors, who'll then offer you notes for that second draft. Contact your local theater director for details.

188 Write a novel.

They say everyone has a book in them. Well, why not you? Whether you fancy writing a mystery, historical novel, science fiction, fantasy, romance, young adult, paranormal, or even graphic novel, you'll find the support you need online . . . or at your local bookstore. So begin!

to wit

When Margaret Edson wrote her first play, she drew upon her experience working in a hospital and her brother's illness. *Wit*, the heartwrenching story of a John Donne scholar dying of ovarian cancer, debuted at the South Coast Repertory in Costa Mesa, California, and went on to Connecticut and New York, winning the Pulitzer Prize in 1999. Emma Thompson starred in the HBO version in 2001.

CALL TO
Online Action!

Top Five Writing Websites
www.writersdigest.com
www.nanowrimo.org
www.mysterywriters.org
www.rwanational.org
www.write4kids.com

189 Learn a new dance.

"Nobody cares if you can't dance well. Just get up and dance."

— DAVE BARRY

Humans dance. And why not? Dancing is good for your soul *and* your body. And here in America you can learn dances born of virtually every tradition—flamenco from Spain, belly dancing from the Middle East, hula dancing from Hawaii, the tango from Argentina, clog dancing from Ireland, and so on. Try ballet, modern dance, or that all-American classic, tap.

TOP SIXTEEN DANCE FILMS

All That Jazz	*Saturday Night Fever*
An American in Paris	*Singing in the Rain*
Chicago	*Step Up*
Dirty Dancing	*Stomp the Yard*
Flashdance	*Swing Time*
Footloose	*Turning Point*
Moulin Rouge	*West Side Story*
Oklahoma!	*White Nights*

▶ The College Entrance Examination Board in 1996 reported that students with experience in musical performance scored 51 points higher on the verbal part of the SAT and 39 points higher on the math section than the national average. In another study, music majors were the most likely group of college grads to be admitted to medical school (66 percent, the highest percentage of any group).

190

Learn to play an instrument.

191 Take a photography class.

Capturing life on film—that's the goal. Taking a photography class can help you learn how to do just that. Whether you want to take better pictures of your grandchildren with your new digital camera, or master the art of black-and-white photography with your 35mm Leica, there's a class for you.

shoot it

Photography is America's number one avocation. According to *Popular Science Monthly*, some 19 million amateur photographers across the nation took some 600 million still pictures last year, spending more than $100 million for film, supplies, and new equipment.

192 Learn to paint.

Watercolor, oils, acrylics . . . the possibilities are endless. Take a class in the medium of your choice—and lose yourself in the canvas.

"Every time I paint a portrait I lose a friend."

—JOHN SINGER SARGENT

193 Throw a pot.

The ancient art of pottery still resonates today. There's nothing like the feel of clay under your fingers or the satisfaction of creating something beautiful and useful from the very earth we walk on. Throw your first pot, and you connect to a tradition nearly as old as humankind itself.

194

Perform at a poetry slam.

195 Learn a lost art.

Your grandfather's whittling. Your grandmother's quilting. Mom's apple pie and Dad's fly tying. Ask your favorite older relative to teach you an art or craft so that your family's artistic traditions survive for generations to come.

196 Teach your art or craft to local schoolchildren.

In the wake of the No Child Left Behind Program, many schools offer far fewer art and music classes. You can help by volunteering to share your artistic talents with students of any and every age.

The arts are critical to every America's education. Even as schools across the nation continue to cut funding for the arts, study after study proves that the arts help kids:

"All children have creative power."

— BRENDA UELAND

★ Boost their academic performance
★ Master critical-thinking, problem-solving, communication, and leadership skills
★ Learn tolerance and open-mindedness
★ Express their feelings in creative ways
★ Increase self-confidence
★ Stay in school

Source: Americans for the Arts

197

Mentor an aspiring artist or writer.

Spend three hours of three days each week for a year mentoring a young person in the arts and that kid is:

> "Every child is an artist. The problem is how to remain an artist once he grows up."
>
> — PABLO PICASSO

★ Four times more likely to be singled out for academic achievement
★ Three times more likely to serve on the student council
★ Four times more likely to be in a math and science fair
★ Three times more likely to be recognized for school attendance
★ Four times more likely to write an award-winning essay or poem

Source: Stanford University

top five poetry collections for children

1. *Mother Goose Nursery Rhymes*
2. *Where the Sidewalk Ends* by Shel Silverstein
3. *A Child's Garden of Verse* by Robert Louis Stevenson
4. *Poetry for Young People* by Maya Angelou
5. Anything by Dr. Seuss

198

Teach a child your favorite poem.

The only thing better than a bedtime story is a bedtime poem . . . or two. Children's poems are fun to read—and the rhythm may even lull your young charge to sleep. Read them often enough, and the kids you read them to will memorize them without even trying.

199 Sing in a choir.

Singing in a choir is not just fun, it's actually good for you. In a three-year study conducted by George Washington University, members participating in the Senior Singers Chorale proved healthier over time than their nonsinging counterparts. In fact, the senior singer groups suffered fewer vision problems, fewer falls, and less depression. They also required far fewer doctor's visits and less medication. So don't just sing in the shower. Join your church choir or your community chorale today—and sing away!

"You always feel better when you sing. Music touches people's hearts."

— JEWEL

200 Take a kid to a local children's museum.

More than 30 million people visit children's museums every year—and you and your favorite child should be among them. According to the Association of Children's Museums, there are 243 such institutions in America—and seventy-eight more on the drawing board. In addition to a wealth of fun and educational exhibits for kids, these wonderful organizations often run afterschool programs, do outreach to local schools, and provide curriculae as well. So take a child to your local children's museum—and learn like a kid again.

top ten children's museums

1. The Children's Museum of Indianapolis
2. The Children's Museum of Houston
3. The Children's Museum, Boston
4. Port Discovery, Baltimore
5. Discovery Center, Rockford, IL
6. Brooklyn Children's Museum
7. Strong Museum, Rochester, NY
8. Minnesota Children's Museum, St. Paul
9. Children's Discovery Museum of San Jose, California
10. Madison Children's Museum, Wisconsin

Source: *www.parents.com*

five plays kids love to play in

1. *How the Camel Got His Hump* by Aurand Harris (based on Rudyard Kipling's *Just So Stories*)
2. *The Three Little Kittens* by June Barr
3. *The Golden Goose* by Paul Sills
4. *Who Laughs Last?* by Nellie McCaslin
5. *Pyramus and Thisbe* by William Shakespeare (adapted from *A Midsummer's Night Dream*)

Source: *Plays Children Love* by Coleman Jennings

201 Start a children's playhouse.

Children love pretend; playacting *is* play for them. Children are natural performers; why not give them a safe place to perform? Set them up to perform at your local church or synagogue, or community center, or even in the backyard. Just remember to clap long and hard.

202 Send a kid to summer music camp.

Music lessons are expensive—and music camps are even more expensive. Often the most talented young musicians lack the resources to attend these highly beneficial opportunities to focus on their music. Find the right one for your favorite little musician at *www.kidscamps.com*.

"If I were not a physicist, I would probably be a musician. I often think in music. I live my daydreams in music. I see my life in terms of music."

—ALBERT EINSTEIN

203 Join your local theater group.

Playacting is not just for kids. Indulge your inner thespian by joining your local theater group. You don't have to be a star to be in the show. You can also paint props, make costumes, do makeup, handle the lights, or run the box office. But whatever you do, you're bound to have fun. Theater groups are typically close communities of like-minded people bound to become your friends. So enjoy the family-like atmosphere—and soak up the world of the stage!

"My love for the theater has always been a priority. That hasn't changed. I got into acting that way. The film work that came up was really a surprise."

— PHILIP SEYMOUR HOFFMAN

204

Join the local photographer's guild.

"There are always two people in every picture: the photographer and the viewer."

— ANSEL ADAMS

205

Host a crafts event at a retirement home.

▶ Crafts for seniors:
Calligraphy
Digital photography
Flower arranging
Homemade greeting cards
Painting
Quilting or sewing
Scrapbooking
Wreath making

Seniors love doing arts and crafts, and will welcome your volunteering to host a crafts event for them. That said, you must keep in mind the physical limitations that plague older people. Arthritis and poor vision, among other ailments, may affect their ability to enjoy some activities. But there are still many arts and crafts that they can do to great effect (see the sidebar for suggestions).

206

Ask your grandmother to teach you to knit.

207

Take a child to a Renaissance Fair.

Knights, dragons, fairies . . . what's not to like? Part amusement park, part performance art, part history lesson, this peculiarly American re-enactment of Olde England was the brainchild of a Southern Californian school teacher named Phyllis Patterson. What began as a class activity in her backyard soon grew into the Renaissance Pleasure Faire. Now there are some 100 fairs held across the nation every year. A lively concoction of jousting and swordplay, music and dancing, artisans and performers, food and frolic, these fairs delight the old and young alike. So don your long dresses and knight's tights, and take your favorite little fairy princesses and knights of the round table to your local fair.

the faire-est of them all

Many well-known actors did their first acting at the famous Renaissance Pleasure Faire in California, most notably:

Rosanna Arquette
Emilio Estevez
Penn Jillette
Charlie Sheen

208

Play in a local band.

Do it for fun or profit or both. Rock, pop, blues, jazz, country, folk, classical, ethnic—the choice is yours. Find a band and sign on, or find some like-minded musicians and start your own. Play local clubs and bars, at proms and bar mitzvahs, weddings and anniversary parties. Or just jam in your garage.

top five garage bands

1. The Black Keys
2. The Kills
3. The Von Bondies
4. The Kings of Leon
5. The Secret Machines

Source: *The Colgate Maroon-News*

209 Support the Cultural Bill of Rights.

In his seminal work *Arts, Inc.: How Greed and Neglect Have Destroyed Our Cultural Rights*, folklorist and musicologist Bill Ivey proposes a Cultural Bill of Rights that would ensure every American's right to an expressive life. Designed to help preserve and sustain American art and culture, this bill would encourage Americans to participate in the arts—and rescue a cultural heritage increasingly threatened by commercialization. As part of Barack Obama's arts and culture transition team, Ivey should be well poised to make sure that the Cultural Bill of Rights sees the light of day in the new administration. Write your congressional representatives in support of this and other efforts to make the arts a priority in the Obama administration.

Rallying Cry!

"We Americans love— even worship—our artists from afar, but once the curtain comes down or, as Bob Dylan says, 'the gallery lights dim,' we're just as happy if they quietly leave the stage. Americans don't take artists very seriously."

— BILL IVEY

Former chairman of the National Endowment for the Arts under the Clinton Administration and member of Obama's arts and culture transition team

210 Host an exhibit for an artist at your workplace.

Art and commerce do not have to be strange bedfellows. You can give talented artists the opportunity to exhibit their work, dress up your workplace with fine art, and endear yourselves to your clients and community by providing exhibit space at your place of business. Line the walls of your lobby, restaurant, or reception area with the work of your favorite local painters, textile and collage artists, and craftspeople. If you don't know any, then check with your local arts association for worthy candidates.

"Promotion and perception are synonymous twins of art marketing."

—JACK WHITE
Of the White Stripes

211 Hire a poet for a creativity workshop at work.

If Linus Pauling was right, and the best way to have a good idea is to have lots of ideas, then what you need is a lot of ideas. That requires creativity, and poets by definition are creative. Bring in a poet to run a creativity workshop for you and your coworkers, and you'll jumpstart the brainstorming process.

THE PRESIDENT SAYS

"When power leads man toward arrogance, poetry reminds him of his limitations. When power narrows the area of man's concern, poetry reminds him of the richness and diversity of existence. When power corrupts, poetry cleanses."

—JOHN F. KENNEDY

212 Become a member of your local museum.

You can support your local museum and feed your soul with a year's worth of art and culture for the (typically) low, low cost of an annual membership. Membership usually offers other benefits as well: invitations to openings and fundraisers, early notice of upcoming exhibits, free or discounted guest passes for your friends and family, even discounts at the museum store. So sign up today!

"I went to the museum where they had all the heads and arms from the statues that are in all the other museums."

—STEVEN WRIGHT

213 Turn an extra room into a studio for an artist.

It's full of junk right now, and has been for years. You know you really don't need that room—and that wasted space could be put to good artistic use. So clean it out and offer it up gratis to your favorite aspiring artist. Even—and especially—if that favorite artist is you!

Rallying Cry!

"A woman must have money and a room of her own if she is to write fiction."

—VIRGINIA WOOLF

214 Swap your own professional services for original artwork.

It's a fair trade: your work for a work of art. If you're a doctor, lawyer, or tax accountant, you can barter your professional services for—to paraphrase Keats—"a thing of beauty that will be a joy forever." Approach the artist of your choice and deal, baby, deal.

"Making money is art and working is art and good business is the best art."

—ANDY WARHOL

215 Host a fundraiser for your favorite arts organization.

Funding for the arts has suffered in recent years—but you can help make up the difference. Put together an event designed to raise money for your preferred arts organization. The more creative, the better. From bachelor auctions and celebrity roasts to putt-putt tournaments and poker nights, there are a wealth of options available for the picking.

top five fundraising events

1. Auctions
2. Dinners
3. Sports tournaments
4. Raffles
5. Trivia nights

216

Donate a product or service as a prize for an auction.

There are no downsides here. Your favorite arts organization gets a prize for its auction, and you get some free promotion, great public relations, and a tax writeoff. What's not to like?

Rallying Cry!

"Art doesn't transform. It just plain forms."

—ROY LICHTENSTEIN

217

Organize an open studios event for an arts community.

The tradition of artists opening their workplaces to art lovers in their communities began in Boston and has now spread across the land. These up-close-and-personal events allow you to visit your favorite artists in the very places where they create their work—inevitably places of creativity, imagination, and magic.

THE PRESIDENT SAYS

"If art is to nourish the roots of our culture, society must set the artist free to follow his vision wherever it takes him."

—JOHN F. KENNEDY

218

Organize a wall mural painting in your community.

> *"I start a picture and I finish it. I don't think about art while I work. I try to think about life."*
>
> —JEAN-MICHEL BASQUIAT
> Graffiti artist turned expressionist

219

Fight to keep art and music education in your local schools.

220 Support the National Endowment for the Arts.

This federal agency, has since its founding in 1965, dedicated itself to bringing art to every state in the nation, awarding more than $3.9 billion to fund projects such as:

★ Artists' residencies in schools
★ Museum exhibitions
★ Internet initiatives
★ Literary fellowships
★ National tours
★ International exchanges
★ Theater festivals
★ Design competitions
★ Folk arts
★ Historic preservation

Although the agency has seen drastic cuts in funding over the past decade, its influence remains indisputable. In fact, every NEA dollar spent generates seven to eight times more in matching grants.

Rallying Cry!

"Because a great country deserves great art."
— NEA SLOGAN

"I see things like they've never been seen before. Art is an accurate statement of the time in which it is made."

— ROBERT MAPPLETHORPE

PART
FIVE

KEEP
AMERICA
COMPASSIONATE

CHAPTER 17

BE KIND TO OUR CHILDREN

163

221.

Help a foster child.

163

222.

Adopt a teenager.

164

223.

Be a Big Brother or Sister.

164

224.

Babysit for a single parent.

164

225.

Volunteer at a local children's hospital.

165

226.

Become a Boy Scout or Girl Scout leader.

165

227.

Play Secret Santa to a disadvantaged child.

166

228.

Join the Make-a-Wish foundation.

167

229.

Be a coach for the Special Olympics.

167

230.

Volunteer for the D.A.R.E. program.

168

CHAPTER 18

BE KIND TO ONE ANOTHER

169

231.

Do one small kindness a day.

169

232.

Give a homeless person your winter coat.

170

233.

Bake a cake for a shut-in.

170

247.

Invest in socially responsible stocks and bonds.

181

248.

Tithe 10 percent of your income.

181

249.

Take a volunteer vacation.

182

250.

Donate to your favorite religious charity.

183

251.

Participate in a fundraising Walk for Hunger.

183

252.

Host a neighborhood watch event.

184

253.

Start a nonprofit organization.

185

BE KIND TO OUR CHILDREN

17

221 Help a foster child.

According to Fostercaremonth.org, if nothing changes by the year 2020, more than 300,000 children will "age out" of the foster care system in poor health and ill-prepared for success in higher education, technical college, or the workforce. Our help is urgently needed. May is Foster Care Month, but those kids need a hand the other eleven months of the year, too! Log on to *www.fostercaremonth.org*, or the National Foster Parent Association (*www.nfpainc.org*) to see what you can do. The Fostercaremonth.org site offers a menu of ways to help, broken down by how much time you have to volunteer: minutes, hours, days, weeks, or more.

in good company

There are an estimated 12 million foster care alumni in the United States representing all walks of life. Behind this startling statistic are countless stories of children who grew up to be thriving adults while others struggled with life's challenges all alone.

Source: *www.fostercarealumni.org*

222 Adopt a teenager.

There are many teenagers in the world that live in orphanages and foster care homes. Usually, couples looking to adopt want a baby or young child, so orphaned teens are often the hardest to place. Open your heart and your home to one.

223 Be a Big Brother or Sister.

Your commitment could have a positive impact on the life of a young person. For example, more than half of the kids with a Big Brother or Big Sister are less inclined to ditch school and roughly 46 percent steer clear of ever using illegal substances. Visit *www.bbbs.org* for information.

224 Babysit for a single parent.

Babysit for a single parent or family in need for free. Childcare costs can be a huge burden and can often stop a single parent from earning their much-needed maximum potential income. If you can offer to help for a couple of hours here and there, you'll be doing a great service.

225 Volunteer at a local children's hospital.

Better yet, involve your children in volunteerism. Since some places may have minimum age requirements for children, you can start getting your children involved at home. Help a child make a flier about a book drive you organize for a children's hospital or low-income daycare. Then, walk with the child to place the fliers in mailboxes in the neighborhood, and donate books neighbors drop off at your house.

THE PRESIDENT SAYS

"We cannot always build the future for our youth, but we can build our youth for the future."

— FRANKLIN DELANO ROOSEVELT

226 Become a Boy Scout or Girl Scout leader.

The mission of the Boy and Girl Scouts of America is "to prepare young people to make ethical and moral choices over their lifetimes by instilling in them the values of the Scout Oath and Law." Scouting makes a positive impact on your community by teaching values and leadership skills to our nation's youth. If you cannot volunteer to become a leader, contribute by joining the individuals, corporations, and foundations who support Scouting's mission. If you haven't had a small child for a while, log on to the national scouting websites and see the vast array of programs offered—they're a national treasure, just like our children.

CALL TO Online Action!

Scout It Out
According to the Boy Scouts of America website, in December 2007, the Boy Scout program membership had 2.8 million youth members and 1.1 million adult leaders. Learn more about their mission, programs, and strategic plan on *www.scouting.org*.

227

Play Secret Santa to a disadvantaged child.

Many local charities offer Secret Santa programs, as do department stores, businesses, and police and fire departments. Call your local Family and Child Services office (listed in the government pages of your local phone book) and ask about opportunities. You can also deliver presents to homeless shelters and women's shelters and many charitable organizations, such as the Salvation Army or Goodwill. When you buy gifts for underprivileged children, include a toy or stuffed animal for little children, as they need a special surprise—and warm clothing.

Also, give globally. The Society of Secret Santas, an anonymous group of leaders throughout the world, performs random acts of kindness to those less fortunate. Using their own financial resources—and without a tax deduction—these leaders share their wealth with those in need. They give from their hearts, remaining forever anonymous. Check them out on *www .secretsanta.com*.

"Believe in love. Believe in magic. Hell, believe in Santa Claus. Believe in others. Believe in yourself. Believe in your dreams. If you don't, who will?"

—JON BON JOVI

"God is a Republican, and Santa Claus is a Democrat."

—HENRY LOUIS MENCKEN

228 Join the Make-a-Wish foundation.

Founded in 1980, this organization has blossomed into a worldwide phenomenon, reaching more than 167,000 children around the world. According to their website, a network of nearly 25,000 volunteers enable the Make-a-Wish Foundation to serve children with life-threatening medical conditions. Volunteers serve as wish granters, fundraisers, and special events assistants. Log onto *www.wish.org* to find your local chapter or make a donation. Maybe you can fulfill someone's wish!

wish granted

171,140 wishes are granted every forty minutes.

Source: Make-a-Wish Foundation

229 Be a coach for the Special Olympics.

Special Olympics is an international non-profit organization that empowers individuals with intellectual disabilities to become physically fit, productive, and respected members of society through sports training and competition in thirty Olympic-type summer and winter sports. If you can't coach, volunteer at the Special Olympics. There are many tasks for volunteers, including serving as drivers, athlete escorts, presenters, scorekeepers, fundraisers, first-aid personnel, and more. Click on the "volunteer" icon at *www.specialolympics.org*.

► The Special Olympics has truly become a global movement, with more than 500,000 athletes in China, more than 210,000 in India, almost 550,000 in the United States, more than 600 in Afghanistan, and 4,400 athletes in Rwanda.

230

Volunteer for the D.A.R.E. program.

CALL TO
Online Action!

D.A.R.E. to Volunteer
The D.A.R.E. program has more than 75,000 trained and certified officers in America. Visit *www.dare.com* to learn more about the program's current initiatives and plans for the future.

"It's so easy for a kid to join a gang, to do drugs . . . we should make it that easy to be involved in football and academics."

— SNOOP DOGG

D.A.R.E. (Drug Abuse Resistance Education) is a police officer–led series of classroom lessons that teaches children from kindergarten through twelfth grade how to resist peer pressure and live productive drug- and violence-free lives. According to their website, millions of D.A.R.E.-educated schoolchildren around the world learn the skills they need to avoid involvement in drugs, gangs, and violence. Founded in 1983 in Los Angeles, it is now being implemented in 75 percent of our nation's school districts and in more than forty-three countries around the world. Help out with this worthy cause by donating time or money at *www.dare.com*.

When it comes to prevention, it's this simple: The D.A.R.E. program works. And not just for illicit drugs, but for smoking as well. A recent study in the *Journal of the National Medical Association* revealed that kids in the D.A.R.E. program are five times less likely to take up smoking than kids who aren't in the program.

BE KIND TO ONE ANOTHER

18

231 Do one small kindness a day.

The truth is that each of us has some power. Aligned with others, we can become a force. We can change the status quo. Make it a random act of kindness, such as:

★ Helping an elderly or infirm person up the stairs or onto a bus
★ Waving a mother with a crying child in front of you in the check-out line
★ Shoveling your neighbor's sidewalk and rushing in before they see you
★ Putting a small vase of flowers on a lonely neighbor's porch
★ Sending a thank-you card to your local police and fire departments (and sending them a homemade cake)

You get the idea!

Rallying Cry!

"A single act of kindness throws out roots in all directions, and the roots spring up and make new trees. The greatest work that kindness does to others is that it makes them kind themselves."

— AMELIA EARHART

232 Give a homeless person your winter coat.

In almost any region, it can get cold at night in the winter. In the northern areas, where it's bitterly cold in the winter, homeless people hardly ever have enough warm clothing to survive. Go through your closets and donate the ones you no longer wear. While you're at it, donate unwanted shoes, sweaters, jeans, and other items that you no longer use to a local shelter or charity. Blankets, boots, shoes, warm socks, hats, gloves, and anything else you can think of will warm someone's heart and body in the cold months.

CALL TO
Online Action!

All Wrapped Up
In 2008, the Salvation Army said, due to the tough economy, its 1,300 thrift shops are receiving fewer donations because customers are keeping their old clothes longer, and making money by selling their clothes on Craigslist and eBay.* Consider forgoing your eBay sale on that coat and donate it instead. Visit *www.goodwill.org* for more information.
*Source: *The New York Times*

233 Bake a cake for a shut-in.

You can really brighten the life of anyone who rarely has opportunities to go outside. Often a simple visit can make a world of difference, but kick it up a notch and bake them a homemade cake. You can go with packaged cakes and they'll be thrilled, or you can bake a cake from scratch, something that may remind them of their mother like an old Midwestern pineapple upside-down cake, or a special little box of Scottish shortbread to savor with a hot cup of tea.

234 Volunteer at a soup kitchen.

Each day, hunger is experienced in every community across this country. As the economy tanks, more and more people will become reliant on soup kitchens, and all associated services, such as food drives and local food banks. Don't wait until Thanksgiving or Christmas (when many people volunteer at soup kitchens); find the organizations in your community that need volunteers and start this week. You can help out in your local community through activities such as:

enough!
In November 2008, the Agriculture Department reported 36.2 million adults and children suffered from hunger during 2007.

★ Repackaging donated food for use at food pantries
★ Serving meals
★ Transporting food to charitable agencies
★ Clerical work

THE PRESIDENT SAYS

Feeding America (formerly known as Second Harvest) feeds more than 25 million neighbors each year. For every $1 you donate, their network helps provide 20 pounds of food and grocery products to men, women, and children facing hunger in our country. Log onto their website and see all the ways you can help: *www.feeding america.org.*

"The war against hunger is truly mankind's war of liberation."
— JOHN F. KENNEDY

235 Drive an elderly neighbor to a doctor's appointment.

Getting to and from appointments may seem mundane to healthy, young, energetic individuals, but it can be a major headache for an elderly person without easily accessible transportation. An elderly neighbor will appreciate your concern, and it would give you both a chance to get to know one another.

enough!
Out of the 37 million people in the world who are blind, the humanitarian organization Orbis asserts that 28 million of them went blind unnecessarily because of lack of treatment and appropriate eye care.

236 Read for the blind.

Help record audio versions of newspapers, books, and magazines for the visually impaired. Check out Recording for the Blind & Dyslexic (*www.rfbd.org*) today and volunteer. Also, support the work of Orbis in aiding the blind. Orbis works to restore the vision of many in the developing world and prevent blindness. See *www.orbis.org*.

"Kindness is a language which the deaf can hear and the blind can see."

— MARK TWAIN

237 Staff a volunteer hotline.

Be a volunteer for a mental health hotline. Give support and comfort to people in their time of great distress. Many times, these people just need someone to talk to. You can be that person. Suicide hotlines and battered women hotlines always need volunteers.

Other hotlines also need help. Consider these two:

"Suicide is a permanent solution to a temporary problem."

— PHIL DONAHUE

1. Al-Anon or Alateen hotlines help those suffering from their parent's, children's, or other family member's alcoholism. Help staff the Al-Anon hotline at 1-888-4-Al-Anon. Find out more about how to be involved with Al-Anon or Alateen at *www.al-anon.alateen.org*.
2. Gay and lesbian hotlines. Help callers who are struggling with fear, depression, or are in some kind of distress as a result of their sexual orientation. The hotline number is 1-888-THE-GLNH; visit *www.glnh.org* for more information.

enough!
A generally accepted statistic is that one person's addiction to alcohol affects four other people. When a parent or teen is drinking, the entire family suffers.

238 Collect donations for a local battered women's shelter.

These women face the monumental task of leaving an abuser and starting a new life. Often they are frightened and poor and have children to support. "Domestic violence does not only happen to adults. Forty percent of girls age 14 to 17 report knowing someone their age who has been hit or beaten by a boyfriend, and approximately one in five female high school students reports being physically and/or sexually abused by a dating partner," according to Senator Dianne Feinstein.

Do whatever you can to offer financial or moral or clothing support. Donate time, money, or household goods. Domestic violence is epidemic in America. If this cause is one that speaks to your passion, help any way you can to stop the violence. Call a women's shelter and find out what it specifically needs. Get friends and family to help you provide what is needed.

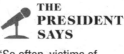

THE PRESIDENT SAYS

"So often, victims of domestic abuse suffer in silence—they don't know where to turn; and they often have no one to turn to. And so it's easy to think that one of these victims could be somebody you love—a mother, a daughter, or a sister. . . . I want you to know that you're not alone in this struggle—that there are people listening and fighting with you to bring this issue out of the darkness of isolation and into the light of justice. I want you to know that I'll continue to be one of those people."

— BARACK OBAMA

BE KIND TO OUR FELLOW CREATURES

239 Build a birdhouse.

According to Birdhouses101.com, more than fifty species of birds like to nest in birdhouses. Birdhouses play an important role in the conservation of birds in heavily populated suburban areas, where very few natural nesting places remain. Providing a mixture of habitats may attract a great number of birds.

You can easily build or buy a bird feeder. After filling it, remember to regularly clean it to avoid spread of avian infections. If you fill your feeder with bird food that attracts songbirds, you'll enjoy listening to the songs of your newfound feathered friends and watching them flock to your feeder at feeding times.

"I once had a sparrow alight upon my shoulder for a moment, while I was hoeing in a village garden, and I felt that I was more distinguished by that circumstance that I should have been by any epaulet I could have worn."

—HENRY DAVID THOREAU

240 Plant a butterfly garden.

Butterflies help pollinate a variety of plants, so support their efforts! Begin by researching which butterflies live in your area and what they may need specifically. You can do this by spending some time outdoors with a field guide to see which species are around, or use a search engine, or try your local library. Plant your butterfly garden in a sunny location (one that receives full sun five to six hours each day), but sheltered from wind. Butterflies won't want to feed in an area where they are constantly fighting the wind to stay on the plants. Place a few flat stones in your sunny location so the butterflies can take a break while warming up. Keep a mud puddle damp in a sunny location, or fill a bucket with sand and enough water to make the sand moist, or provide water in a birdbath or fountain.

that's a lot of butterflies

According to the North American Butterfly Association, the world has approximately 20,000 butterfly species. Around 100 species of butterflies can be found near your home in most parts of the United States.

"I grew up on Tarzan movies and Jacques Cousteau documentaries— that fostered an early love for wildlife and the wilderness and subsequently survival."

—LES STROUD
Host of *Survivorman*

241 Feed wildlife in the winter.

Leave out seeds, nuts, and other food that may appeal to the local wildlife. This will help those not hibernating survive in the dead of winter, when the ground is frozen and they can't find seeds and berries as easily.

242 Boycott products tested on animals.

Although efforts have been made to reduce and eliminate animal testing, it is still the primary method of providing data on most cosmetics. Its continued use is partly based on the familiarity with the protocols and data analysis. To find cruelty-free cosmetics, look for the leaping bunny logo. The leaping bunny symbol is awarded by the Coalition for Consumer Information on Cosmetics, an organization made up of eight national animal rights groups. The coalition works with companies to promote nonanimal testing and is making progress in the United States and overseas. Their shopping guide is available online at *www .leapingbunny.org/shopping_guide.htm.*

CALL TO
Online Action!

Contact the FDA
Visit *www.fda.gov/com ments.html* to e-mail the FDA about your feelings on animal testing. While the plight of animals used in laboratory testing can be emotional, be sure to emphasize the accuracy and availability of alternative measures. You should also include any applicable laws and regulations pertaining to the issue.

enough!

According to the Humane Society of the United States, roughly 2 to 4 million animals in the United States are used to test the safety of chemicals and consumer products in laboratories.

243 Volunteer at a local animal rescue center.

We all know that thousands of animals are languishing in animal rescue centers. Call your local animal rescue organization and offer them whatever skills you have, which could range from helping with physical care, editing a newsletter, designing a radio or TV ad campaign, or brainstorming fund-raising ideas. See *www.hsus.org* for more information.

(not) enough!

Dogs adopted from animal shelters represent 10 percent of all owned dogs; cats adopted from animal shelters represent 18 percent of all owned cats.

Source: American Pet Products Manufacturers Association's 2007–2008 National Pet Owners Survey

244 Save a bird.

According to *www.stfranciswildlife.org,* if you observe what appears to be an abandoned baby bird outside its nest, unless it's in a dangerous area, watch for an hour or two to see if the mother will return. If she doesn't and you can't find the nest, cut drainage holes in a small container, add grass, and use wire to attach it to the shady side of a tree or bush. Check it periodically, from a distance, to make sure the parents return.

If the baby bird is hurt and its parents don't return, move the makeshift nest to a quiet place, but do *not* attempt to give it food or water. Birds breathe through a hole in their tongues, and water placed in its mouth will be inhaled.

Juvenile birds, identifiable by their immature feathers and short tails, may hop around on the ground in a covered area near their nest for several days; that's normal. Fully feathered birds should be left alone. Don't put them back in the nest, as they're likely to jump out again and may hurt themselves. This is their normal order of business: Parents protect and feed them on the ground until they can fly.

bird myth

It is a myth that once you touch a baby bird the parents will not accept it back into the nest. Birds do not have a well-developed sense of smell.

"I hope you love birds too. It is economical. It saves going to heaven."

—EMILY DICKINSON

245
Be a foster caregiver for a pet.

If you cannot adopt, but you could provide interim shelter, food, and veterinarian care for an animal, consider being a foster care provider for your local animal shelter. Or you can help by donating to the Humane Action Network, a grassroots organization seeking legal protections for animals against cruel treatment and suffering. See *www.hsus.org* for more information.

THE PRESIDENT SAYS

"Most shelter dogs are mutts like me."

—BARACK OBAMA

246
Spay or neuter your cats and dogs.

Spaying and neutering animals reduces the growing populations of stray dogs and cats and can have an added benefit of reducing the possibility of humans being bitten by such animals infected with rabies. If you don't have a dog or cat, make a donation to an animal sterilization clinic. Look into organizations like Spay Neuter Assistance Program (SNAP) or the American Society for the Prevention of Cruelty to Animals (ASPCA). Through spay/neuter clinics on wheels, such organizations usually offer services free or at reduced fees to low-income families receiving public assistance such as Food Stamps. To find out more, go to *www.spayusa.org* or *www.aspca.org*.

"It is in the nature of cats to do a certain amount of unescorted roaming."

—ADLAI STEVENSON

SUPPORT GOOD WORKS

247 Invest in socially responsible stocks and bonds.

Practice socially responsible investing. Companies like Equal Exchange are letting you put your saved money to good use, and get it back! (Visit *www.equalexchange.com/eecd* for more information.) To learn more about socially responsible investing including a very detailed analysis of various options, visit *www.socialfunds.com*.

248 Tithe 10 percent of your income.

Donate it to your church or favorite local charity. If you have the money and can spare some for others who have none, consider making a tithing commitment.

"October. This is one of the peculiarly dangerous months to speculate in stocks in. The others are July, January, September, April, November, May, March, June, December, August, and February."

— MARK TWAIN

249

Take a volunteer vacation.

Even though they do cost travel expenses and sometimes a little more, why not spend your time off helping others? There are a multitude of choices these days, including the standbys like Habitat for Humanity. You can go on adventures that range from an archaeological dig abroad or working at the Gettysburg Civil War Park. Team up with an organization like the Sierra Club (*www.sierraclub.org*) and go out on a service trip. The reward of seeing the faces of those people whose lives you've brightened will be compensation enough.

Look in your local library or bookstore to find resource books chock-full of ideas. You can also search on the Internet, but *always* verify that they are legitimate businesses before sending any money. A few to view as a jumping-off place:

★ Charityguide.org
★ Globalvolunteers.org
★ Transitionsabroad.com
★ Away.com

250 Donate to your favorite religious charity.

As a community organizer, our new president saw up close how faith and values could serve a community. "I believe that change comes not from the top down, but from the bottom up, and few are closer to the people than our churches, synagogues, temples, and mosques," President Barack Obama said on the campaign trail.

▶ Another idea: Go global and serve as an unofficial ambassador abroad by signing up for a religious mission overseas. Check with your local house of worship to see if they're planning on sending any volunteer groups overseas.

251 Participate in a fundraising Walk for Hunger.

Project Bread's Walk for Hunger in Boston is the oldest continual pledge walk in the country. It raises millions of dollars each year in privately donated funds to assist more than 400 emergency food programs in 126 communities statewide. Project Bread also advocates systemic solutions that prevent hunger and that provide food to families in everyday settings, including schools. Over the last four years, the organization has invested more than $2 million in grants to community organizations that feed children where they live, learn, and play. Many cities and communities have begun their own Walks for Hunger. If you can't find one in your community, start one—or fund one in another city or state.

(not) enough!
Project Bread raised an estimated $3.8 million for emergency programs across Massachusetts, when more than 40,000 people participated in its 2008 Walk for Hunger. They will likely need more than $4 million for the coming year.

Rallying Cry!

"It's easy to make a buck. It's a lot tougher to make a difference."

—TOM BROKAW

"The impersonal hand of government can never replace the helping hand of a neighbor."

—HUBERT H. HUMPHREY

252 Host a neighborhood watch event.

Host a "neighborhood watch" event with your local police. Invite your neighbors to learn what each of you can do to keep your neighborhood safe from crime. Call your local police department for details. Also, make a master list of the names, addresses, and phone numbers of every family living on your street or in your condo or apartment complex. Offer to give each family a copy. Let everyone know that the list is for letting other neighbors know when suspicious activity (such as vandalism or a possible break-in) occurs at one or more of the houses on the street.

Also, help protect your neighborhood and your neighbors in other ways. After you secure your home from a tornado or hurricane, offer to help a neighbor put up hurricane shutters before the storm hits. Thorough storm preparation can make a big difference.

253

Start a nonprofit organization.

As President Obama just proved in his groundbreaking win, grassroots organizations can take fire overnight. If you have needs in your community that you feel passionately about, or a fabulous idea for a creative cooperative venture that could generate funds to support numerous charities, consider starting your own nonprofit organization. You can always start small and expand as supporters come on board. All the information you'll need to get started is available on *www.usa.gov* (search for nonprofit) or on *www.nonprofit.about.com*. Do your homework first, but by all means, get started. Bring your unique talents and drive to the table, and *yes, you can* make a difference.

For more resources, try these websites:

★ Nonprofitlaw.com and Managementhelp .org have information on incorporating, drafting a business plan, raising funds, and building a board.
★ Research existing nonprofits at Guidestar.org.
★ Find organizations that provide funds for nonprofits at Foundationcenter.org.

"Spontaneous combustion of grassroots politics is the future. "

—DICK MORRIS

by the numbers

According to the National Center for Charitable Statistics, as of January 2006, 850,455 public charities and 104,276 private foundations were registered with the IRS.

PART
SIX

KEEP
AMERICA
HEALTHY

267.

Pair up with a buddy to exercise three times a week.

199

268.

Walk for a cure.

200

269.

Start a lunch walk group at work.

200

270.

Walk your dog.

201

271.

Take up a new sport.

201

272.

Go dancing every Saturday night.

202

273.

Build a playground in your neighborhood.

203

274.

Take up yoga.

203

275.

Coach a kids' sports team.

204

276.

Play a team sport.

204

277.

Send a kid to sports camp.

205

278.

Take a fitness vacation.

205

279.

Swim.

206

280.

Join your local gym or YMCA.

206

CHAPTER 23

SAVE A LIFE— INCLUDING YOURS

207

281.
Become an organ donor.

207

282.
Learn CPR.

283.
Hold CPR training.

208

284.
Reduce your risk of heart disease.

209

285.
Lose 10 percent of your excess body weight.

209

286.
Quit smoking.

210

287.
Get health insurance.

211

288.
Get a flu shot.

212

289.
Go to the dentist twice a year.

212

290.
Take a self-defense class.

213

291.
Practice emergency preparedness.

213

292.
Donate blood.

214

293.
Wear your seatbelt.

214

294.
Wear your helmet.

215

295.
Learn to meditate.

215

296.
Laugh.

216

EAT RIGHT

CALL TO
Online Action!

Campaign to rid local schools of vending machines.

254

Obesity rates continue to rise in the United States. Since 1980, being overweight has doubled in children and tripled in adolescents. The Clinton Foundation, the American Heart Association, and the nation's three biggest beverage manufacturers—Coke, Pepsi, and Cadbury Schweppes—agreed to begin rolling back their presence in schools. Beginning now and progressing through the 2009–10 school year, the manufacturers will kick high-calorie, sugary drinks out of school vending machines and replace them with bottled water, unsweetened fruit juices, low-fat milk, and sugar-free sodas. Log on to the National Conferences of Legislature for information on vending machines in your school district: *www.ncsl.org/programs/health/Child hoodObesity-2005.htm.*

Get Involved
Federal regulations recommend parent involvement in their school's cafeteria. The School Nutrition Association's website, *www.school nutrition.org,* offers tips for having a productive discussion with your school's food service director.

enough!
In 2000, 43 percent of elementary schools, 89.4 percent of middle/junior high schools, and 98.2 percent of senior high schools had a vending machine or a school store, canteen, or snack bar where students could purchase [unhealthy] foods or beverages.

Source: Centers for Disease Control and Prevention's School Health Policies and Programs Study

255 Bag your lunch.

Planning meals will benefit your wallet and your waistline, so create nutritious and delicious meals the night before—for you and your children. Also, to be environmentally conscious, avoid using disposable bags or containers. Find inexpensive lunchbags, plastic bottles, and containers that you can reuse—ditto for the kids' lunchbags.

▶ The Food and Drug Administration is so convinced of soy's benefits that the agency approved a health claim for soy protein and heart disease in October 1999. Good sources include defattened soy flour, isolated soy protein, firm tofu, soy cheese, regular tofu, soymilk, and soy veggie burgers. Adding one serving a day can make a difference.

256 Make Tofu Surprise once a week.

According to experts, soy protein appears to help prevent heart disease by lowering blood cholesterol levels; decreasing blood clots and platelet "clumping" or aggregation (both of which can increase the risk for a heart attack or stroke); improving the elasticity of arteries (which makes blood flow better); and reducing oxidation of low-density lipoprotein (LDL or "bad" cholesterol), which can lower the risk of plaque formation. Researchers suspect that the beneficial effects from soy protein are due to the isoflavones, but more research is needed. Whether or not it's the isoflavones in the soy that are helping prevent heart disease remains to be seen, but the protective benefits of soy are tremendous. Soy up!

257 Know your cholesterol numbers.

Ask your doctor for a total lipoprotein profile so that you are aware of not only your total cholesterol, but of each component of your cholesterol. You may have a total cholesterol level that is desirable, but that doesn't mean your HDL and LDL levels are in line. Your total cholesterol level will fall into one of three categories:

★ *Desirable:* less than 200 mg/dL
★ *Borderline high risk:* 200–239 mg/dL
★ *High risk:* 240 mg/dL and over

If you fall within the borderline high-risk range, you have at least twice the risk of a heart attack compared with someone in the desirable range. If you are in this range, your HDL is less than 40 mg/dL, and you don't have other risk factors for heart disease, you should have your total cholesterol and HDL rechecked in one to two years. You should also lower your intake of foods high in saturated fat and cholesterol. Your doctor may order another blood test to measure your LDL cholesterol. Even if your total cholesterol puts you in the borderline high-risk range, you may not be at high risk for a heart attack. Some people can have high HDL-cholesterol and desirable LDL levels, so it is best to ask your doctor to interpret your results.

enough!
Every year in the United States, nearly a quarter million people die within one hour of having a heart attack, mostly due to arrhythmias.

► With 16 percent of children and adolescents age six to nineteen overweight (that equals 9 million children), childhood obesity remains a pressing public health concern.

► The Environmental Defense Fund rates which fish are eco-friendly and which are not. Eco-friendly fish are those whose fishing or farming methods have minor impact on the environment, and eco-unfriendly fish are those whose capture causes considerable impact on the environment. Log onto *www .edf.org* for all the information you'll ever need on which are the safest fish to eat and also which ones cause the least damage to our environment. Tip: Eat a variety of fish to minimize high-mercury content.

258 Eat breakfast.

After a good night's rest, your body needs to replenish its blood sugar stores—its main source of energy. Your brain in particular needs a fresh supply of glucose each day because that is its main source of energy, and it does not store it. Probably because of that fact, eating breakfast is associated with being more productive and efficient in the morning hours. Breakfast eaters tend to experience better concentration, problem-solving ability, strength, and endurance. Your muscles also rely on a fresh supply of blood glucose for physical activity throughout the day.

259 Eat more fish.

Fish is a miracle food. Most fish (when not deep-fried) are low in calories and low in those "bad" unsaturated fats and they contain oodles of those omega-3 "good" fats that protect your brain and your heart. Since the human body can't make significant amounts of these essential nutrients, fish are an important part of the diet. Eating fish also has positive benefits for our environment: Farming fish is far less impactful than farming cattle.

260 Eat more fruit.

Fruit is full of healthy substances such as vitamin C, vitamin A, potassium, folic acid, antioxidants, phytochemicals, and fiber, just to name a few. Citrus fruits, berries, and melons are excellent sources of vitamin C. Dried fruits are available all year long and are an excellent source of many nutrients including fiber. Almost all fruits and vegetables are good for you, but some are better than others. When it comes to fruit, apples, bananas, berries, citrus fruit, and melons are your best bets because of their high fiber and nutrient content.

▶ Here are a few easy and healthy suggestions for adding fruit to your breakfast:

- Cold cereal with fruit and skim milk
- Yogurt with fruit or low-fat granola cereal
- Peanut butter on a whole-wheat bagel and orange juice
- Bran muffin and a banana
- Instant oatmeal with raisins or berries
- Breakfast smoothie (blend fruit and skim milk)
- Hardboiled egg and grapefruit juice

261 Eat more veggies.

Daily requirements for several vitamins—including vitamin C; folic acid; and beta-carotene, the precursor for vitamin A—can be met almost exclusively from fresh vegetables and fruits. This is especially true with dark-green leafy vegetables, such as spinach or broccoli, and dark orange vegetables, such as carrots or yams. Some vegetables also supply sufficient amounts of calcium, iron, and magnesium. Vegetables also contain compounds called phytochemicals that may provide additional health benefits.

another reason to eat veggies

Cruciferous vegetables are rich in cancer-preventing antioxidants (as well as other healthful benefits). The most potent cruciferous vegetables include bok choy (Chinese cabbage), broccoli, Brussels sprouts, cabbage, cauliflower, collard greens, kale, mustard greens, rutabagas, turnips, and watercress.

262 Replace red wine with a blueberry smoothie.

We all know that red wine has antioxidants that benefit our heart health, and it can help you relax at the end of a busy day, but did you know that blueberries have far more antioxidants? Blueberries are, in fact, a superfood. One cup of blueberries reportedly provides three to five times more antioxidants than five servings of carrots, broccoli, squash, and apples. This can give you a lower risk of heart disease, vibrant skin, and a boost in brainpower.

► A report published in the *Journal of Agriculture and Food Chemistry* showed that the blueberry has 38 percent more antioxidants than red wine.

263 Swear off fast food.

Ever since Bill Clinton swore off fast food (after he had to have a heart bypass), he's been far slimmer and trimmer. And now we have a new, slim, trim, and athletic president that may inspire millions to swear off fast food! If you didn't see *Super Size Me*, one viewing will cure you of any cravings. Although you can buy salads at many fast food restaurants now, it's far more likely—let's be honest here—that you're ordering something fried and loaded with saturated fat and excess calories. Do your waistline and your heart a favor and eschew fast food restaurants.

enough!

A ban on fast-food advertising to children would cut the national obesity rate by as much as 18 percent, according to a new study conducted by the National Bureau of Economic Research and funded by the National Institutes of Health.

264 Teach your kids to cook.

Not only will this bolster family time away from video games or lethargically watching television, it's fun. And better yet, it will teach your children extremely valuable skills that will put them on the path to healthy eating for the rest of their lives. Use the time to teach them about healthy food choices, healthy portions, healthy ingredients—and the joy of cooking. As we all know from past experience, if you don't know how to cook when you graduate from college or move out of Mom's and Dad's home, you are far more likely to graze, or, worse yet, rely on fast food for a large portion of your "diet." Cooking with your kids is a win-win situation, so strap on the aprons (make customized aprons together!) and get cooking!

265 Sit down to dinner every night.

A recent survey by the National Center on Addiction and Substance Abuse (CASA) at Columbia University titled "The Importance of Family Dinners," revealed a strong correlation between frequent family dinners and reduced risk that a teen will smoke, drink, or use illegal drugs.

CALL TO Online Action!

Now You're Cooking
Check out *www.recipe ladies.com/kidscooking .html* for hundreds (literally) of ideas and recipes! A Disney site, *www.family fun.go.com/recipes/kids*, has a special section for how to encourage picky eaters to cook and eat healthier foods.

Rallying Cry!

"Children and adolescents who have family meals are likely to eat more vegetables and fruit, consumer fewer soft drinks, and consume more calcium, iron, and fiber."

—DR. MARY STORY
The School of Public Health at the University of Minnesota

266

Master the art of low-fat cooking.

Oils, salad dressings, cream, butter, gravy, margarine, cream cheese, soft drinks, candy, jams, gelatins, and fruit drinks supply calories and fat but little in the way of nutrients.

▶ Note: Some fats, such as flaxseed oil, peanut butter, and avocados, are "good" fats when used in moderation. When cooking, make daily low-fat choices.

★ Choose low-fat or fat-free dairy products such as skim milk; 1-percent milk; low-fat cheese, sour cream, and yogurt; and reduced-fat ice cream.

★ Buy low-fat dressings and use those that are higher in saturated fats, such as buttermilk ranch or blue cheese, less often.

★ Use nonstick cooking sprays or nonstick pans instead of frying with large amounts of oil or butter.

★ Look at food labels for amounts of total fat and types of fat.

★ Watch for hidden fats in your foods, such as toppings on pizza, fried foods, ice cream, high-fat meats (salami, bologna, bratwurst, hot dogs, pepperoni, sausage, bacon, and spare ribs), cakes, cookies, macaroni salad, potato salad, and coleslaw.

★ Limit your intake of red meat, especially higher-fat cuts. Opt for poultry, fish, or nonmeat dishes more often.

★ Watch for ingredient lists and fat content on margarines.

now you see it, now you don't

With cooking oils, try to buy the least processed/refined oils you can afford, and use them sparingly. Plus, be aware that when you see an oil—particularly soybean oil—listed in processed foods, make sure the word *hydrogenated* doesn't precede it.

KEEP ACTIVE

Pair up with a buddy to exercise three times a week.

267

We drive instead of walk. We call people instead of walking over to their houses. We use leaf blowers, riding lawn mowers, and power tools. We use escalators instead of stairs. This rise in inactivity has been devastating to our health. We have witnessed the meaning of the "use it or lose it" phenomenon. The bottom line: We are meant to be active, and our health depends upon it. When the body is used, it thrives; when it isn't, it merely survives. Rally a friend to join you in getting off the couch and doing something—anything—that moves your body. Most experts agree than thirty minutes of aerobic exercise three times a week can make a real difference.

enough!

Americans watch an average of more than four hours of TV a day, or two full months of TV a year. According to Dr. William Dietz, Director of the Division of Nutrition and Physical Activity at the Centers for Disease Control, "The easiest way to reduce inactivity is to turn off the TV set."

 THE PRESIDENT SAYS

"Physical fitness is not only one of the most important keys to a healthy body, it is the basis of dynamic and creative intellectual activity."

— JOHN F. KENNEDY

THE PRESIDENT SAYS

"I walk slowly, but I never walk backward."

—ABRAHAM LINCOLN

► In 1900, the leading causes of death in the United States were not at all related to lifestyle, but were instead diseases and infections that science eventually conquered—pneumonia, tuberculosis, gastroenteritis, and influenza. Today, the leading causes of death are heart disease, stroke, cancer, and accidents.

268 Walk for a cure.

Ever since the Susan G. Komen Race for the Cure began attracting hundreds of thousands of men, women, and children participating in walks to raise money to raise awareness and seek a cure for breast cancer, virtually every disease has a "walk for the cure" event. Type in "walk for a cure" on Google.com for hundreds of options. Choose your favorite and call friends and family to join you. And if you can't find a walk in your area, go to the respective websites and make a donation. Then, consider how much you could help by establishing a walk in your hometown.

269 Start a lunch walk group at work.

Sitting in chairs all day creates problems. The position they force your body into shortens some muscles (those in the front of the body) and lengthens others (those in the back of the body), which creates an imbalance leading to pain and injury. Lunchtime is the perfect time to stretch your body and burn some calories. Find a group of like-minded coworkers and make a pact to take a walk during your lunch hour, preferably outside to get fresh air.

270 Walk your dog.

And if you don't have a dog, volunteer to walk your neighbor's dog, or dogs in your local pound. The dogs will love you forever, and you'll get in shape and relieve stress. There's nothing like doggie kisses to bring a smile to your face.

271 Take up a new sport.

Most of us have one activity that we center our exercise schedules around. What your body needs, however, is variety, or cross-training. Cross-training means that you are working different muscles and improving overall physical strength and conditioning. Taking up a new sport will add an important balance to your activities, providing increased cardio, strength, *and* mind-body/flexibility. For example, if you walk for exercise, take up swimming or tennis or volleyball or mountain climbing or ice skating or bicycling—or dancing (see entry 272)! If you're not a sporting enthusiast, consider adding workouts three times a week. Walking is a great cardiovascular workout, but if you add strength training, such as weight training or yoga, you'll improve your overall health—and probably lose weight, as well.

THE PRESIDENT SAYS

"If a dog will not come to you after he has looked you in the face, you should go home and examine your conscience."

—WOODROW WILSON

"In every walk with nature one receives far more than he seeks."

—JOHN MUIR

1952 vs. 2008

Women today eat an average of 2,178 calories a day, but only burn off 556 through daily activities. In 1952, the average woman ate 1,818 calories a day and burned 1,512 calories.

Rallying Cry!

272 Go dancing every Saturday night.

Dancing can get you into shape, and it's
a great way to be social. But you can also
dance by yourself at home with just the
radio on. Here's a list of different dance
styles, their benefits, and their calorie-
burning count for a moderate intensity for
thirty minutes:

★ *Ballroom dancing:* Burns 150 calories
  an hour. Strengthens leg, shoulder, ab,
  arm, back, and glute muscles; increases
  flexibility. Improves concentration. Only
  increases heart strength if you do fast
  steps, such as swing dancing.
★ *Salsa dancing:* Burns 170 calories an
  hour. Strengthens leg, shoulder, ab, arm,
  back, and glute muscles. Also increases
  flexibility. Strengthens the heart.
★ *Ballet:* Burns 150 calories per hour.
  Strengthens leg, shoulder, ab, arm, back,
  and glute muscles. Also increases flexibility. You need concentration and stam-
  ina. Does not increase cardio power.
★ *Country line dancing:* Burns 125 calories
  an hour. Strengthens leg, shoulder, ab,
  arm, back, and glute muscles.
★ *Disco dancing:* Burns 175 calories an
  hour. Strengthens leg, shoulder, ab, arm,
  back, and glute muscles. Strengthens
  the heart.

273

Build a playground in your neighborhood.

274 Take up yoga.

Everyone can do yoga regardless of age, size, flexibility, or health. Many people unfamiliar with yoga think that they have to be like a Gumby toy—able to touch their toes to their nose—but this is not true. Overweight people, pregnant women, and older people can practice yoga and receive its benefits. There are many types of yoga suitable for anyone and poses can *always* be modified to fit an individual's needs. Yoga is fabulous for men and women alike. Not only does it help you stretch and elongate muscles, it helps you learn to breath more efficiently, and clear your mind through meditation and focused relaxation. It's one of the most potent workouts you can do, good for the heart, and good for your sex life. So grab a mat and find a class.

"Basketball is an endurance sport, and you have to learn to control your breath; that's the essence of yoga, too. So, I began using yoga techniques in my practice and playing. I think yoga helped reduce the injuries I suffered."

— KAREEM ABDUL-JABBAR

275 Coach a kids' sports team.

Until just a few years ago, kids were the best example adults had for what an active, fit life should look like. Unfortunately, between video games, long rides (rather than walks) to school, and slashes in school budgets for gym and athletics, kids have become the new face—or body—of the growing obesity problem. While boys are more prone to play team sports, they tend to spend too much time playing video games. For them, and for girls, too, there's a huge advantage to playing a sport. Call your local parks and recreation office to find out how you can get involved.

276 Play a team sport.

THE PRESIDENT SAYS

"I wish to preach, not the doctrine of ignoble ease, but the doctrine of the strenuous life."

— THEODORE ROOSEVELT

Our new president loves to relax and stay fit by playing basketball. Team sports are not only a great way to stay active—and young—they also strengthen friendships, role model the importance of staying active to your children, and improve your health. And they're fun stress-busters. You can find adult leagues in your area—look for the traditional sports like softball, soccer, and tag football, or try some unique ones, like kickball, Ultimate Frisbee, or dodgeball.

277 Send a kid to sports camp.

Just imagine how many American children would love to go to a summer camp, but never get the opportunity because their parents simply cannot afford it. You can give a gift that will last a lifetime. If you don't know any children, call your local schools or government offices and offer a "scholarship" for one, or more, children to attend the camp of your, or their, choice. Visit *www.camping.about.com* for a mega-list of adventure camps.

"I see great things in baseball. It's our game—the American game."

— WALT WHITMAN

278 Take a fitness vacation.

Traveling to a new destination coupled with being active is an exciting combination. How about running a 10k event in Hawaii or Florida? What about bicycling across your favorite state or European country? You could walk inn-to-inn in Spain or France. Consider other options: resorts with activities (skiing, swimming, and skating); walking vacations; biking trips; hiking treks; and far more adventurous options, such as mountain climbing, backwoods cross-country snowshoeing, kayaking, trips during which you learn to sail, and other skill-focused trips.

► Here are just a few destination events:

- **Bay to Breakers, San Francisco, CA**
- **Peachtree Road Race, Atlanta, GA**
- **Gasparilla Distance Classic, Tampa, FL**
- **Bike Ride Around Lake Tahoe, Lake Tahoe, CA**
- **Run to the Far Side, San Francisco, CA**

THE PRESIDENT SAYS

"It is good to realize that if love and peace can prevail on earth, and if we can teach our children to honor nature's gifts, the joys and beauties of the outdoors will be here forever."

— JIMMY CARTER

279 Swim.

While most sports have just a few benefits and lack others (walking, for example, doesn't increase flexibility or build strength in the upper body), swimming is very close to perfect, although it doesn't build bone. However, swimming works your whole body, improving cardiovascular conditioning, muscle strength, endurance, posture, and flexibility all at the same time. Your cardiovascular system in particular benefits because swimming improves your body's use of oxygen without overworking your heart. So be like Michael Phelps and swim, baby, swim.

Gold Gym's top ten fittest presidents

1. John Quincy Adams
2. George W. Bush
3. Gerald Ford
4. Jimmy Carter
5. Theodore Roosevelt
6. Harry S. Truman
7. Zachary Taylor
8. Thomas Jefferson
9. Herbert Hoover
10. George Washington

280

Join your local gym or YMCA.

SAVE A LIFE— INCLUDING YOURS

281 Become an organ donor.

People from all walks of life spend hours, days, months, and years waiting for transplant organs. Types of organs that are most often required included heart, lungs, kidneys, pancreas, and liver. Also needed are tissues such as skin, heart valves, intestines, corneas, bones, and tendons. Find out more about how to give the gift of life at *www.organdonor.gov*.

You can also give the gift of sight. Make a donation of any size to *www.sightsavers .org*. Your generosity could pay for a cataract operation on an adult to restore his or her sight. A little bit more might buy a microscope for a hospital or train eye care workers.

a long wait

There are more than 100,000 people waiting for an organ transplant in the United States alone, according to the United Network for Organ Sharing.

"The only gift is a portion of thyself."

— RALPH WALDO EMERSON

282 Learn CPR.

Courses are offered through local community colleges, park and recreation departments, and local branches of the Red Cross. You can even learn CPR from a video that has been approved for home training by the American Heart Association. Check out *www.cpr-training-classes.com* to sign up.

▶ If you remember that 1970s Bee Gees hit, "Staying Alive," you could save a life. According to a University of Illinois College of Medicine study, the disco tune's beat is right in rhythm with the rate of chest compressions needed when giving CPR.

"I always believe in being prepared, even when I'm dressed in white tie and tails."

— GENERAL GEORGE S. PATTON

283 Hold CPR training.

Consider holding CPR training at your workplace or during a meeting of your local community group. The American Heart Association is an excellent resource, but your local fire department may also be available to offer training. Also, encourage your management to lobby for a portable defibrillator for your office, and urge them to train everyone how to use it, as well.

284

Reduce your risk of heart disease.

Several nutritional factors are important in helping to prevent heart disease. To reduce the impact of the controllable risk factors for heart disease, the American Heart Association recommends the following dietary and lifestyle goals:

★ Eliminate cigarette smoking.
★ Consume appropriate level of calories and exercise to prevent obesity.
★ Eat a heart-healthy diet.
★ Do not consume more than two alcoholic drinks (1 to 2 ounces) per day.

▶ Other recommendations include consuming at least 25 to 30 grams of fiber each day from sources such as whole grains, fruits, vegetables, and legumes. Consuming a variety of fruits and vegetables will also ensure that you receive plenty of beta-carotene, vitamin C, folic acid, vitamin E, and other antioxidants and protective substances such as flavonoids and carotenoids. Talk to your doctor about your risk for heart disease and how to manage any risk factors you may have.

285

Lose 10 percent of your excess body weight.

Losing just 5 to 10 percent of excess body weight can help reduce your risk for health problems related to your weight and help lower blood pressure, total cholesterol, LDL cholesterol (bad cholesterol), triglyceride levels, and blood sugar. Lifestyle change is the healthiest and most permanent method. Combining a healthy diet with increased physical activity and behavior modification is the most successful strategy for healthy weight loss and weight maintenance.

"If you haven't got any charity in your heart, you have the worst kind of heart trouble."

— BOB HOPE

286 Quit smoking.

body, heal thyself

Our bodies begin repairing the damage to our respiratory system within days of that last cigarette. Unless you already have cancer or emphysema, the health of your lungs (and other organs adversely affected by tobacco, such as the heart) will continue to improve until, finally, you're almost as well as before you took that first puff.

Nicotine dependence is the number one chemical dependence in the United States and is as addictive as cocaine, heroine, and alcohol. Smoking may cause premature death from heart disease, stroke, and cancer, and yet the tobacco companies aggressively market their products not only to rich countries but also to developing nations.

Take heart in knowing that our new president is also battling a cigarette addiction—and winning. Hop on board the stop-smoking train and do whatever you have to do to vastly improve your health by simply not lighting up. Of course it's hard, but you can do it!

Also urge your friends to kick their habit. Share the dangerous facts about smoking. Find out more at *www.cdc.gov/tobacco/data_statistics/Factsheets/cessation2.htm*.

"If we see you smoking we will assume you are on fire and take appropriate action."

—DOUGLAS ADAMS

287 Get health insurance.

Not having health insurance can be catastrophic. Studies have shown that those without insurance fall into certain patterns, some of which are:

1. They are more often diagnosed much later, which results in a higher risk of mortality.
2. Workers and their families that are not insured don't go for regular medical checkups, don't go to doctors, or make use of prescriptions, settling for over-the-counter medicine, even in cases where more advanced medication is needed.
3. A large proportion of uninsured people use emergency care as their only medical facility. Some wait until they truly are critical, and others use these very expensive services for illnesses that could be treated without hospitals, incurring tremendous expense and crowding emergency rooms.

It has been estimated recently that 47 million Americans don't have health insurance. This leaves vast numbers of our citizens in peril, as well as placing severe strain on hospitals and the national budget. Do your part and research ways that you can acquire health insurance.

THE PRESIDENT SAYS

"In a country as wealthy as ours, for us to have people who are going bankrupt because they can't pay their medical bills—for my mother to die of cancer at the age of 53 and have to spend the last months of her life in the hospital room arguing with insurance companies because they're saying that this may be a pre-existing condition and they don't have to pay her treatment, there's something fundamentally wrong about that."

— BARACK OBAMA

▶ Many states offer assistance for low-income families. If all else fails, consider "catastrophic" coverage, also known as High-Deductible Health Plans (HDHPs), that will cover expenses once they reach a certain point, such as $2,000 or more. Even if it's a strain on your budget, having a "catastrophic" policy will protect you from financial ruin.

▶ Flu shots are especially important for:

- **Children ages six to twenty-three months**
- **Adults and children with chronic heart and lung disease**
- **Anyone living in a nursing home or chronic care facility**
- **People sixty-five years of age and older**
- **People with chronic conditions such as diabetes, anemia, cancer, immune suppression, HIV, or kidney disease**
- **Health care workers, along with other caregivers and household contacts capable of transmitting influenza to the above at-risk groups**

enough!

Among parents whose children needed dental care but didn't get it, more than half said it was because of cost or not having dental insurance.

288 Get a flu shot.

Flu shots are very safe for the majority of people and can save individuals six to ten days of perfect misery and workplaces hundreds of hours of lost productivity. Do it for yourself, but do it for your family, your friends, and your coworkers, too. Certain groups *should not* be vaccinated. These include children under six months of age and people who have had a severe allergic reaction to eggs or to a previous dose of the vaccine.

289 Go to the dentist twice a year.

Seeing your dentist twice a year for a checkup and cleaning can vastly improve your dental health and help prevent tooth decay and gum disease. Here's a short list of what you can do every day to keep your mouth and teeth healthy:

★ Brush your teeth every day with a fluoride toothpaste.
★ Floss your teeth every day.
★ Snack smart—limit sugary snacks.
★ Get enough calcium.
★ Don't smoke or chew tobacco.

290 Take a self-defense class.

Prevention is key to protecting yourself. You don't need a gun—arm yourself with knowledge. Log onto *www.safetyfor women.com* to view an extensive (and fabulous) laundry list of tips to raise your self-defense consciousness. Use the list to educate yourself, your friends, and your children. Or, take a boxing or karate class to bolster your strength and increase your sense that you can take care of yourself—if you have to. This confidence is often relayed subconsciously, which means you'll repel those seeking to exploit or harm you.

enough!

According to *www.self defenseresource.com*:

- 5.2 million violent crimes and 18.7 million property crimes occurred in 2004 in the United States.
- Every 2.5 minutes a sexual assault is committed somewhere in America.
- About 44 percent of rape victims are under age eighteen, and 80 percent are under age thirty.

291 Practice emergency preparedness.

FEMA's website offers *Are You Ready? An In-Depth Guide to Citizen Preparedness* (IS-22), a comprehensive resource on individual, family, and community preparedness. The guide provides a step-by-step approach to disaster preparedness by walking the reader through how to get informed about local emergency plans, how to identify hazards that affect their local area, and how to develop and maintain an emergency communications plan and disaster supplies kit.

▶ Download *Are You Ready?* for free from *www.fema.gov/are youready*. Or write to them for a free copy:

Federal Emergency
  Management Agency
P.O. Box 2012
Jessup, MD 20794-2012

292 Donate blood.

A blood donation equals one pint of blood. The average adult body has ten to twelve pints at any given time. The vast majority of people will not feel any different. A small percentage may experience temporary dizziness, but rest and fluids will help you feel better quickly. Your body will replace the lost fluid within twenty-four hours. The whole process takes about an hour. It starts with registration, a health history, and a miniphysical. Then comes the actual donation, which usually takes approximately ten to twelve minutes. Afterward, you will be asked to spend a few minutes in the "canteen" to enjoy a light refreshment before returning to your normal activities.

Give Blood!
To learn more about blood donation opportunities, visit *www.givelife.org* or call 1-800-GIVE-LIFE (1-800-448-3543). If you have questions or concerns about safety or whether you will be able to donate, visit *www .givelife2.org/donor/faq .asp*, where you'll find answers to all your questions.

"We make a living by what we do, but we make a life by what we give."

— WINSTON CHURCHILL

293 Wear your seatbelt.

Ever since they were made mandatory in all vehicles, seatbelts have saved thousands of lives and prevented many more serious injuries. Every time you get behind the wheel, make sure those you are driving put on their seatbelts, too. Teach your children to wear seatbelts, and reinforce its importance as they reach the age where they will be riding in cars with friends.

294 Wear your helmet.

When you hit your head and go unconscious, you are likely bruised and bleeding in there. If you are unconscious for more than an hour from a head injury, you run twice the risk of developing Alzheimer's. It's imperative that you wear a helmet when riding a motorcycle, but skateboarding, bicycling, hockey, football, and rock climbing are all sports that encourage participants to wear helmets.

enough!

It's been estimated that 75 percent of all bicycling deaths result from brain injury.

295 Learn to meditate.

Stop rushing and turn inward in contemplation and meditation. It's good for your body and mind. It helps you achieve clarity in thinking and deal with emotional stress. Meditation comes in many forms, including sitting meditation, walking meditation, mindfulness meditation, yoga meditation, and even prayer. You don't need a class, or one "right" way to do it. Simply create time and space to sit or lie still, slow down your mind, and begin slowly tuning out the world and quieting your senses. As you relax, feel yourself sinking deeper into the quiet until you begin to feel inner peace, and then linger there for at least ten minutes.

► **Bonus: Meditation also works to train the mind to avoid negative patterns and thought processes, vicious circles of failure and low self-esteem, even the perception of chronic pain as an intensely negative experience.**

296 Laugh.

Laugh out loud. Laugh loud, laugh often, and get others to laugh with you. Laughter releases enzymes in the human brain that can bring about new learning. Laughter also benefits the heart, improves oxygen flow to the brain, and works the muscles in the head, neck, chest, and pelvis—in much the same way as the stress reduction exercises of yoga. This helps keep muscles loose and limber and enables them to rest more easily. So rent a funny movie, go to a comedy club, or watch a comedy show, and laugh! For starters, check out AFI's top ten funniest movies of all time:

1. *Some Like It Hot*
2. *Tootsie*
3. *Dr. Strangelove*
4. *Annie Hall*
5. *Duck Soup*
6. *Blazing Saddles*
7. *M*A*S*H*
8. *It Happened One Night*
9. *The Graduate*
10. *Airplane!*

Source: American Film Institute

the science of laughter

Laughter helps lower serum cortisol levels, increases the amount of activated T lymphocytes, increases the number and activity of natural killer cells, and increases the number of T cells that have helper/suppressor receptors. In other words, a major stress reliever!

Source: Researchers at Loma Linda University School of Medicine's Department of Clinical Immunology

"Laughter is inner jogging."

— NORMAN COUSINS

KEEP
AMERICA
STRONG

CHAPTER 24 **SUPPORT OUR MILITARY**	**297.** Send a care package to a U.S. soldier in Iraq.	**298.** Entertain the troops.
223	223	223
299. Join the National Guard.	**300.** Donate your old cell phones to U.S. soldiers.	**301.** Buy a sailor a ship-to-shore phone card to call home.
224	224	225
302. Volunteer at a veteran's hospital.	**303.** Host a Welcome Home party.	**304.** Donate your frequent flyer miles.
225	225	226
305. Donate a laptop to a wounded soldier.	**306.** Encourage a local group to adopt a platoon.	**307.** Write a letter to "Any Soldier."
226	226	227
308. Say "thank you" to a soldier.	**309.** Wear a poppy on Memorial Day.	**310.** Fly your flag on all patriotic holidays.
227	227	228

311.

Honor a soldier's grave with flowers or a wreath.

228

CHAPTER 25

PRESERVE AMERICA'S HISTORY

229

312.

Join your local historical society.

229

313.

Watch the re-enactment of a famous U.S. battle.

229

314.

Start an oral history project for your community.

230

315.

Research your family tree.

230

316.

Throw a Fourth of July party.

230

317.

Make a documentary about a local historical event.

231

318.

Help a daycare center celebrate Thanksgiving.

231

319.

Visit a national monument or memorial.

231

320.

Take your kids to your state's capital.

232

321.

Accompany a class on a field trip to Washington, D.C.

232

322.

Be a docent at your local historical site.

232

323.

Read a book by Stephen Ambrose or Doris Kearns Goodwin.

233

324.

Watch a documentary by Ken Burns.

233

CHAPTER 26 **CELEBRATE OUR DIVERSITY** 235	**325.** Help prepare an immigrant for his or her citizenship exam. 235	**326.** Teach an immigrant English. 235
327. Learn to speak Spanish. 236	**328.** Celebrate diversity in your workplace. 236	**329.** Throw a Cinco de Mayo party. 236
330. Attend an ethnic festival. 237	**331.** Host a "Melting Potluck" and invite friends to bring regional dishes. 237	**332.** Spend a day in Chinatown. 238
333. Try a new ethnic restaurant. 238	**334.** Learn to cook an ethnic cuisine. 238	**335.** Read a book about the gay experience. 239
336. Join an interfaith council. 239	**337.** Visit another part of the country. 240	**CHAPTER 27** **SPREAD GOODWILL** 241

338.

Serve in the Peace Corps.

241

339.

Invite a foreign student to live with you.

241

340.

Spend your junior year abroad.

242

341.

Collect Pennies for Peace.

242

342.

Invite a foreign friend over for Thanksgiving.

242

343.

Volunteer to be a translator.

243

344.

Watch a foreign film.

243

345.

Be a good ambassador when you travel abroad.

243

346.

Stay at B&Bs and hostels when you travel.

244

347.

Swap homes with a foreign family for vacation.

244

348.

Blog about your travels abroad.

244

349.

Join your local Alliance Française.

245

350.

Learn the language *before* you go.

245

351.

Learn the local customs *before* you go.

245

352.

Watch BBC America and other foreign channels.

246

CHAPTER 28	**353.**	**354.**
GET INVOLVED!	Stay informed.	Report criminal activity.
247	247	248
355.	**356.**	**357.**
Be a good witness.	Serve on a jury.	Honor a good Samaritan.
248	248	249
358.	**359.**	**360.**
Make a speech.	Campaign for your favorite politician.	Encourage others to vote.
249	249	250
361.	**362.**	**363.**
Drive an elderly person to the polls.	Attend a rally.	Join the Citizens Corps Council.
250	250	251
364.	**365.**	
Vote in *every* election.	Run for office.	
251	251	

297 Send a care package to a U.S. soldier in Iraq.

One of the easiest ways to send a care package to a U.S. soldier in Iraq is to donate money to Operation USO Care Package. Since the USO started the program in 2003, the organization has sent more than 1.3 million care packages to our servicemen and -women across the globe—some 25,000 packages a month!

298 Entertain the troops.

Noncelebrity professional entertainers can contact the Armed Forces Entertainment (AFE). The AFE puts on 1,200 shows each year, entertaining servicemen and -women at 270 military installations across the globe. For information, call 1-800-458-0868 or *www.armedforcesentertainment.com.*

what's in a USO care package?

Donate $25, and the USO will send out a $75 care package to a serviceman or -woman. Every care package offers at least:

- A personalized message of support from you the donor
- An AT&T prepaid international phone card
- Snacks
- Playing cards
- Reading material
- Camo kits containing shampoo, conditioner, sunblock, hand sanitizer, toothpaste, and toothbrush

The USO also fulfills requests from deployed units on a first-come, first-served basis.

Source: *www.uso.org*

299 Join the National Guard.

The National Guard traces its roots back to the Massachusetts Bay Colony, which started the first state militia in 1636. Now Guard members serve across America and around the globe; you'll find them wherever our nation needs them, from the flooded streets of New Orleans to the frontlines of Iraq and Afghanistan.

300 Donate your old cell phones to U.S. soldiers.

Americans stick some 130 million old cell phones in drawers every year. There's a better way. Donate your old cell phone to Cell Phones for Soldiers, where teenagers Robbie and Brittany Bergquist will recycle it and use the money to buy prepaid phone cards for soldiers serving overseas. This teenaged brother-sister team from Norwell, Massachusetts, started Cell Phones for Soldiers with $21 of their own money—and have since raised some $2 million, distributing more than 500,000 cards to military personnel around the world. Fish out that cell phone, and drop it off at any AT&T store, or check out *www.cellphonesforsoldiers.com* for a prepaid shipping label.

301 Buy a sailor a ship-to-shore phone card to call home.

Through the Department of Defense Military Exchanges, you can buy a $20 prepaid phone card servicemen and -women can use on board Navy ships and Coast Guard cutters. Check out this link for more info: *https://thor.aafes.com/scs/.*

302 Volunteer at a veteran's hospital.

There are 7.8 million veterans enrolled in the VA Health Care System—nearly 3 million of whom are on disability. Volunteer at a local VA Hospital, and you can give back to those who have given so much for our country. Contact the VA Volunteer Service at *www.volunteer.va.gov* for information.

303 Host a Welcome Home party.

Throw a party on your own for your favorite returning serviceman or -woman, or contact Welcome Home Troops and volunteer to serve as an Event Host. Contact *www .usawelcomehometroops.org* for information.

who are our veterans?

- There are 25 million veterans living in America today.
- Three out of four served during an "official period of hostility," according to the Veterans' Administration.
- Nearly two million are women.

Source: Department of Veteran Affairs

THE PRESIDENT SAYS

"History teaches that war begins when governments believe the price of aggression is cheap."

—RONALD REAGAN

"The troops appreciate beef jerky, sunflower seeds, movies . . . In the outlying areas, they appreciate receiving baby wipes and socks and hygiene products—and all this is topped off with tons of cookies."

—IDA HAGGS
Founder of Adopt a Platoon

304 Donate your frequent flyer miles.

Your frequent flyer miles can be used by families of wounded soldiers so that they can visit them in the hospital. Check out Operation Hero Miles at *www.heromiles.org*.

305 Donate a laptop to a wounded soldier.

LaptopsForTheWounded.com is "a non-profit organization with a goal to provide laptop computers with webcams for the wounded military personnel in hospitals, so they can have access to family and friends when they cannot be there with them." Visit their website to learn more.

306 Encourage a local group to adopt a platoon.

Get your favorite group of like-minded people to adopt a platoon or company of some fifteen to forty servicemen and -women. Once or twice a month you collect care package items, cards, and letters from your group members, which you then wrap up and mail. Contact *www.adoptaplatoon.org* for more information.

307

Write a letter to "Any Soldier."

CALL TO
Online Action!

Letter-Writing Campaign
Visit *www.anysoldier.com* to read more about how this program began and how it works.

308 Say "thank you" to a soldier.

You'll see servicemen and -women on active duty at airports, bus stations, and train stations—and when you do, stop and tell them just how much you appreciate their service. You'll be glad you did.

309

Wear a poppy on Memorial Day.

"In Flanders fields the poppies blow; Between the crosses, row on row . . ."

— COLONEL JOHN MCCRAE

From the poem "In Flanders Fields" that inspired the wearing of poppies on Memorial Day

310

Fly your flag on all patriotic holidays.

Consider the words of Henry Ward Beecher: "Our flag means all that our fathers meant in the Revolutionary War. It means all that the Declaration of Independence meant. It means justice. It means liberty. It means happiness. . . . Every color means liberty. Every thread means liberty. Every star and stripe means liberty."

311

Honor a soldier's grave with flowers or a wreath.

PRESERVE AMERICA'S HISTORY

312

Join your local historical society.

313

Watch the re-enactment of a famous U.S. battle.

From the "shot heard round the world" to the rallying cry "Remember the Alamo!," you can watch the re-enactment of our nation's most memorable battles. Every year, hundreds of such re-enactments take place from coast to coast, many at national parks; contact your local living history society for details. Plus: You can participate in re-enactments as well!

THE PRESIDENT SAYS

"Four score and seven years ago our fathers brought forth on this continent, a new nation, conceived in Liberty, and dedicated to the proposition that all men are created equal.

— ABRAHAM LINCOLN

Gettysburg, Pennsylvania, November 19, 1863

CALL TO
Online Action!

Top Five Battlefield and Re-enactment Sites
1. *www.nps.gov*
2. *www.sutler.net*
3. *www.civilwartraveler.com*
4. *www.reenactorsnetwork.com*
5. *www.nrlhf.org*

Start an oral history project for your community.

CALL TO
Online Action!

Top Five Oral History Websites
1. *www.storycorps.net*
2. *www.oralhistory.org*
3. *www.loc.gov/vets/ vets-home.html*
4. *www.h-net.org/ ~oralhist/*
5. *www.oraltradition.org*

Saving the stories of our American people starts at home. Record the oral histories of the elderly members of your family. For more information, contact your local university, many of which host regional oral history centers, or contact one of the "Top Five Oral History Websites," at left.

"There is no greater agony than bearing an untold story inside you."

— MAYA ANGELOU

Research your family tree.

Thanks to the wealth of online resources now available, tracing your roots has never been easier. As a nation of immigrants, it behooves us to know we came from, who we are now, and where we are going.

CALL TO
Online Action!

Top Five Genealogy Websites
1. *www.ancestry.com*
2. *www.geneaology .com*
3. *www.RootsWeb.com*
4. *www.FamilySearch .org*
5. *www.OneGreat Family.com*

316

Throw a Fourth of July party.

317 Make a documentary about a local historical event.

All you need is a videocamera and an event to document. When you're finished, hold a screening and invite the local hoi polloi. You can also enter your video in one of the many contests for aspiring documentary producers; check out *www.vidopp.com* for listings.

top five documentary contests

1. Hometown Video Awards
2. YouTube Project: Report
3. Sparky Awards
4. C-Span Student Cam
5. Politube

318 Help a daycare center celebrate Thanksgiving.

You can roast a turkey, create costumes for the kids, help them do arts and crafts in keeping with the Thanksgiving theme, and more. Contact your local daycare center and volunteer today.

319 Visit a national monument or memorial.

The next time you find yourself worrying about the state of America today, go visit one of our glorious monuments or memorials. You'll be reminded why you're proud to call yourself an American.

top ten national monuments and memorials

1. White House
2. Statue of Liberty
3. Grand Canyon
4. Washington Monument
5. Mount Rushmore
6. Muir Woods National Monument
7. Booker T. Washington Memorial
8. Lincoln Memorial
9. Aztec ruins
10. Mount St. Helens National Volcanic Monument

320

Take your kids to your state's capital.

321 Accompany a class on a field trip to Washington, D.C.

More than 16 million people visit our nation's capital every year—and many of them are high school students. Contact your local high school—and volunteer to chaperone on their next trip. You can also help raise the money to send the kids on this one-in-a-lifetime educational, fun experience.

322 Be a docent at your local historical site.

Run tours as a docent at your local historical site, and you'll not only learn all about your hometown heritage, you'll also meet interesting people from all over the country—and even the world.

323

Read a book by Stephen Ambrose or Doris Kearns Goodwin.

Lose yourself in the great stories of our nation, as told by two of our most popular historians. You'll learn much about our American past—and the learning will go down very easy. Try Ambrose's *Band of Brothers: E Company, 506th Regiment, 101st Airborne from Normandy to Hitler's Eagle's Nest* or *Undaunted Courage: Meriwether Lewis, Thomas Jefferson, and the Opening of the American West*. Or check out Goodwin's *Team of Rivals: The Political Genius of Abraham Lincoln* or *No Ordinary Time: Franklin and Eleanor Roosevelt: The Home Front in World War II*.

"I've always tried to be fair to my subjects. That's easy when they are as likable and admirable as Lewis and Clark, or Eisenhower."

—STEPHEN AMBROSE

"Once a president gets to the White House, the only audience that is left that really matters is history."

—DORIS KEARNS GOODWIN

324

Watch a documentary by Ken Burns.

Master of the modern documentary, Ken Burns uses archival footage and photographs to bring the history of our nation to life. His films are so rich and moving, it's practically un-American not to watch them. According to Burns, "In a sense I've made the same film over and over again. In all of them I've asked, 'Who are we as Americans?'"

top five Ken Burns films

1. *The Civil War*
2. *Baseball*
3. *The War*
4. *Jazz*
5. *Brooklyn Bridge*

CELEBRATE OUR DIVERSITY

325
Help prepare an immigrant for his or her citizenship exam.

Last year more than a million people pledged their allegiance to the United States of America—but they had to pass a test first. Help an immigrant pass this critical exam, which consists of 100 written questions on American history, government, and democratic principles, along with an English oral, reading, and writing test and ten additional civics questions.

326
Teach an immigrant English.

Volunteer to tutor a non-English speaking immigrant to speak what many consider to be one of the hardest languages to master. That's right, English, which at more than 1,000,000 words boasts the richest vocabulary of any tongue on earth.

could you pass the test?

In October 2008, a revised and updated citizenship test designed to focus on American values and democratic principles went into effect. Here are some sample questions from the new test: Can you answer them all?

1. Name one war fought by the United States in the 1900s.
2. There were thirteen original states. Name three.
3. What does the judicial branch do?

Stumped? Find some of the answers at *www.uscis.gov*.

Source: United States Immigration Support

327 Learn to speak Spanish.

After English, more Americans—31 million of them—speak Spanish at home than any other language.

328 Celebrate diversity in your workplace.

Push for hiring more women and people of color. Crusade for equal insurance benefits for gay and lesbian partners. And fight to keep older Americans on the job unless and until they decide to retire.

THE PRESIDENT SAYS

"As the child of a black man and white woman, born in the melting pot of Hawaii, with a sister who is half-Indonesian, but who is usually mistaken for Mexican, and a brother-in-law and niece of Chinese descent, I never had the option of restricting my loyalties on the basis of race or measuring my worth on the basis of tribe."

— BARACK OBAMA

329 Throw a Cinco de Mayo party.

Join in the annual American celebration of all things Mexican. Hold your own bash at home, hang out at your favorite Mexican restaurant, or attend one of the many festivals commemorating the victory of Mexican forces over the invading French at the Battle of Puebla in 1862. Ironically, celebrating Cinco de Mayo (the fifth of May) is far more widespread in America than it is in Mexico.

330 Attend an ethnic festival.

There are thousands of festivals every year in America; every community has its cultural events, each reflecting the ethnic and regional heritage of its citizens. Most are a grand opportunity to steep yourself in the great food, music, and traditions of another culture. So go, and enjoy!

331

Host a "Melting Potluck" and invite friends to bring regional dishes.

top ten festivals

1. Mardi Gras in New Orleans
2. Aloha Festival in Hawaii
3. St. Patrick's Day Parade in Boston
4. Ullr Fest in Breckenridge, CO
5. Callo Ocho in Miami
6. San Gennaro Festival in New York City's Little Italy
7. Golden Dragon Parade in Los Angeles
8. German Village Oktoberfest in Columbus, OH
9. Highland County Maple Festival in Highland County, VA
10. Martin Luther King March and Rally in Atlanta

 **THE PRESIDENT SAYS**

"We become not a melting pot but a beautiful mosaic. Different people, different beliefs, different yearnings, different hopes, different dreams."

— JIMMY CARTER

332

Spend a day in Chinatown.

333 Try a new ethnic restaurant.

One of the best things about living in a multicultural society: the food!

334 Learn to cook an ethnic cuisine.

Just as fun as eating ethnic food is learning to make it yourself. Ask a friend to show you how to prepare his or her favorite regional dish—or sign up for a class at your local cooking school or gourmet cooking store.

► Salsa has now replaced ketchup as America's most popular condiment.

335

Read a book about the gay experience.

Try *And the Band Played On* by Randy Shilts or *Rubyfruit Jungle* by Rita Mae Brown.

From *Rubyfruit Jungle*: I wished I could be that frog back at Ep's old pond. I wished I could get up in the morning and look at the day the way I used to when I was a child. I wished I could walk down the streets and not hear those constant, abrasive sounds from the mouths of the opposite sex. Damn, I wished the world would let me be myself. But I knew better on all counts.

From *And the Band Played On*: **Before.** It was to be the word that defined the permanent demarcation in the lives of millions of Americans, particularly those citizens of the United States who were gay. There was life after the epidemic. And there were fond recollections of the times before.

"Labels are for filing. Labels are for clothing. Labels are not for people."

— MARTINA NAVRATILOVA

336

Join an interfaith council.

THE PRESIDENT SAYS

"If we cannot now end our differences, at least we can help make the world safe for diversity."

— JOHN F. KENNEDY

337 Visit another part of the country.

Despite the outcry against the so-called homogenization of America, there are still plenty of unique regions to explore. Ours is a big nation—and it will take a lifetime to see it all. Start now. And if you don't want to miss anything, drive.

You don't have to take a lot of time off to travel to another part of our great nation. Given our hectic lifestyles, more Americans are taking weekend trips—rather than longer holidays. More than half of us go on a minimum of one weekend trip every year. Weekend vacations are easier to plan, which may be why 42 percent of weekend travelers make plans at the last minute, and don't even choose a destination until two weeks before the trip. According the Travel Industry Association, the top weekend destinations are:

1. Cities
2. Small towns
3. Beaches
4. Mountain areas
5. Lake areas
6. State or national parks
7. Theme or amusement parks

Source: Travel Industry Association

top ten scenic routes in America

1. Blue Ridge Parkway
2. Hana Highway
3. Highway 1
4. Highway 12
5. Going-to-the-Sun Road
6. Million Dollar Highway
7. Red Rock Scenic Byway
8. Seward Highway
9. Sonoma and Napa Valleys
10. U.S. Route 1

Source: Shermans Travel

"Whither goest thou, America, in thy shiny car in the night?"

—JACK KEROUAC

SPREAD GOODWILL

338 Serve in the Peace Corps.

Join the nearly 8,000 Peace Corps volunteers in seventy-six countries doing "the toughest job you'll ever love." And if you think it's a job for the young, think again. Five percent are over fifty; the oldest Peace Corps volunteer is eighty-four.

"It's better to send in the Peace Corps than the Marine Corps."

—TED KENNEDY

339 Invite a foreign student to live with you.

There's no better way to show the world what America is really like than opening your home—to one foreigner at a time. You can sign up for a number of exchange programs placing students from around the world.

CALL TO Online Action!

Top Five Foreign Exchange Websites
www.pax.org
www.hostanexchange
    student.com
www.AYUSA.org
www.student-exchange-
    alliance.org
www.aifs.com

340

Spend your junior year abroad.

341 Collect Pennies for Peace.

In 1993, mountain climber Greg Mortenson tumbled into a Muslim village in Pakistan, exhausted and weak. The villagers nursed him back to health, and in return he's built seventy-four schools in Pakistan and Afghanistan. One of his fundraising efforts is Pennies for Peace, which encourages American schoolchildren to collect pennies to buy pencils for Mortenson's schools. See *www.penniesforpeace.org* for more.

342 Invite a foreign friend over for Thanksgiving.

How better to introduce strangers in our land to the "real America" than by inviting them to share in our national meal, eat our national bird, and watch our national pastime (with all due respect to baseball)?

343 Volunteer to be a translator.

According to the U.S. Census, 311 languages are spoken in the United States. Some 162 of these are indigenous languages and 149 are immigrant languages. Consider serving as a translator. Organizations such as police departments, hospitals, ESL departments in high schools and colleges, even online digital libraries all need translators, so volunteer today.

"Every great film should seem new every time you see it."

—ROGER EBERT

344 Watch a foreign film.

There's no better way to understand another culture than by spending a little time in that world—and that's what foreign films allow us to do.

345

Be a good ambassador when you travel abroad.

twenty must-see foreign films

All about My Mother
Amelie
Antonia's Line
La Cage Aux Folles
City of God
Crouching Tiger, Hidden Dragon
The Diving Bell and the Butterfly
La Dolce Vita
Fanny and Alexander
The Gods Must Be Crazy
Life Is Beautiful
Like Water for Chocolate
Monsoon Wedding
The Motorcycle Diaries
Pan's Labyrinth
Il Postino
Ran
Run Lola Run
La Vie en Rose
Whale Rider

346 Stay at B&Bs and hostels when you travel.

Swap the formality of the hotel for the warm charm of the bed and breakfast, or the camaraderie of the hostel. You'll meet more interesting people, experience more of the local color, and save money, too.

347 Swap homes with a foreign family for vacation.

It's an inexpensive way to see your preferred destination up close and personal— ditto for the family you swap with. Check out *www.homeexchange.com* (immortalized in the movie *The Holiday*) and sign up for your house trade today.

348 Blog about your travels abroad.

Blogging is the next best thing to being there. You can share your insights and observations with your friends and family every step of your journey by using your own computer, or by stopping in at cybercafés along the way.

349

Join your local Alliance Française.

350 Learn the language *before* you go.

At least learn enough to say the five most important things you need to know when traveling abroad (see sidebar at right).

▶ Five important words and phrases to learn before you travel:

1. Hello
2. Please
3. Thank you
4. Where is the restroom?
5. What a beautiful country!

351 Learn the local customs *before* you go.

Forget Milledgeville. Study up on your destination's cultural mores and traditions in advance of your journey; know the terrain you'll traverse before you set foot on foreign soil.

352

Watch BBC America and other foreign channels.

> *"You've got to turn off the Spanish television set. You're just forced to speak English, and that just makes you learn the language faster."*
>
> — ARNOLD SCHWARZENEGGER
> Addressing the Association of Hispanic Journalists

With the advent of cable television, the American public now has access to many foreign-language channels; there are at least fifteen commercial Spanish TV channels alone. So put that remote to good use; flip through the channels until you find one where you don't speak the language, and watch a while. Or find a channel where they're speaking a foreign language you're trying to master, and watch a while. Either way, you'll learn something. Foreign television continues to attract American viewers, as evidenced by the following statistics from Nielsen:

★ Telemundo is the fastest growing Spanish-language network in America
★ Univision is the most watched Spanish-language channel in America
★ BBC America is the most watched cable network for college-educated Americans aged 25 to 54
★ BBC America is the fifth most popular cable network for Americans 25 to 54 whose household income tops $150,000
★ The number of Asian and Hispanic TV households are growing three times faster than the total number of TV households in America

GET INVOLVED!

353 Stay informed.

It only stands to reason that the better informed we are, the smarter citizens we'll be, and by extension, the smarter country we'll be. Unfortunately, studies show that we are not that well informed:

★ Just 40 percent of Americans can name our three branches of government.
★ 60 percent of young voters under twenty-four cannot find Iraq on a map.
★ Only 49 percent of Americans understand that the only nation ever to employ a nuclear weapon during wartime is the United States.

So make it your civic goal this year to inform yourself. And be an equal-opportunity informee—listen to all points of view before you form your own opinions. You may be surprised what you learn.

Bill O'Reilly versus Jon Stewart

Who's smarter—the conservatives who watch *The O'Reilly Factor* or the liberals who prefer *The Daily Show*? According to a Pew study, 54 percent of *both* show's viewers rank as "high knowledge" citizens.

"You've got stoned slackers watching your dopey show every night and they can vote."

— BILL O'REILLY
When addressing *Daily Show* host Jon Stewart

"This is hot cocoa, I'm going to give you some marshmallows. . . . You're in a safe place. . . . You've got a no-spin zone, I've got a safe zone."

— JON STEWART
When addressing *O'Reilly Factor* host Bill O'Reilly

354 Report criminal activity.

If this seems obvious to you, think again. More than half of all crimes go unreported: 52 percent of violent crime and 62 percent of property crime are *not* reported to law enforcement. Yet, crime is responsible for more death, injury, and property loss than all our natural disasters combined. So if you are witness to or victim of a crime, report it immediately.

"Obviously crime pays, or there'd be no crime."

—G. GORDON LIDDY

THE PRESIDENT SAYS

"I am not a crook."

—RICHARD M. NIXON

355 Be a good witness.

Swear to tell the truth, the whole truth, and nothing but the truth—then do precisely that.

who's serving?

- 5 million Americans report for jury duty as summoned every year.
- 1 million Americans actually serve on a jury every year.

Source: National Center for State Courts

356 Serve on a jury.

A whopping 58 percent of all Americans believe that jury duty is a privilege they enjoy fulfilling, according to a study by the American Bar Association. Odds are, you're one of them. (If you are not, you should be.) So when you receive that summons, welcome the opportunity to participate in our justice system.

357 Honor a good Samaritan.

There are many ways to recognize the good Samaritans among us. Nominate your favorite do-gooders for local community service awards, send out press releases publicizing their good efforts, hold dinners in their honor, organize letter-writing campaigns on their behalf. Or just say, "Thank you."

358 Make a speech.

Exercise your First Amendment rights. It's what makes America *America,* and Americans *Americans.*

359

Campaign for your favorite politician.

360 Encourage others to vote.

The more active Americans are in the running of their country, the stronger our democracy. Ergo: The more Americans engaged in the political process, the better. Double ergo: The more Americans who vote, the better.

361 Drive an elderly person to the polls.

In the early twentieth century, you couldn't offer someone a ride to the voting booth without possibly risking a violation of the Corrupt Practices Act. Now, an army of city buses, minivans, and even limos are commandeered by local governments and political organizations to ensure that the poor, elderly, disabled, and student populations all make it to the polls. You can join one of these efforts, or just offer a ride to a neighbor without one.

THE PRESIDENT SAYS

"I like the noise of democracy."

—JAMES BUCHANAN

362

Attend a rally.

363 Join the Citizens Corps Council.

Join the Citizen Corps, and you join an organization dedicated to first aid and emergency training, first responder support, disaster relief, and community safety. There are 2,339 councils throughout the land that serve 223,906,854 people—a whopping 78 percent of Americans. Check out *www.citizencorps.gov* and sign up today.

364 Vote in *every* election.

Whether you're voting for your hometown's next mayor or the next president of the United States, cast your vote. Just do it.

365 Run for office.

You know what they say: If you want something done right, do it yourself.

THE PRESIDENT SAYS

"We must work toward the day when citizen service is the common expectation and common experience of every American."

— BILL CLINTON

"Hell, I never vote for anybody, I always vote against."

— W. C. FIELDS

THE PRESIDENT SAYS

"And so, my fellow Americans: ask not what your country can do for you—ask what you can do for your country. My fellow citizens of the world: ask not what America will do for you, but what together we can do for the freedom of man."

— JOHN F. KENNEDY

"Yes, we can.

"America, we have come so far. We have seen so much. But there is so much more to do. So tonight, let us ask ourselves—if our children should live to see the next century; if my daughters should be so lucky to live as long as Ann Nixon Cooper, what change will they see? What progress will we have made?

"This is our chance to answer that call. This is our moment.

"This is our time, to put our people back to work and open doors of opportunity for our kids; to restore prosperity and promote the cause of peace; to reclaim the American dream and reaffirm that fundamental truth, that, out of many, we are one; that while we breathe, we hope. And where we are met with cynicism and doubts and those who tell us that we can't, we will respond with that timeless creed that sums up the spirit of a people: Yes, we can.

"Thank you. God bless you. And may God bless the United States of America."

— BARACK OBAMA